The Windows 95® Version of

The Business Strategy and Policy Game

David L. Eldredge
Murray State University
Murray, Kentucky

James R. Marshall
California State Polytechnic University
Pomona, California

Abolhassan Halati
California State Polytechnic University
Pomona, California

C R E D R CORPORATION
CREATIVE EDUCATION DEVELOPMENT RESEARCH

Printed in the United States of America

10 9 8 7 6 5 4 3 2

ISBN 1-893187-00-4

CREDR Corporation

CreativeEducationDevelopmentResearch
Post Office Box 49938, Los Angeles, California 90049
Telephone: 562.696.1610   e-mail: jmarshall@csupomona.edu   www.CREDR.COM

To Judy, Lynn, and Tracey,
who give meaning to the pursuit
of such endeavors
David Eldredge

To Jo Jane for her encouragement
and enthusiastic support
Jim Marshall

To my family for allowing me the time
such projects require
Hassan Halati

Preface to the Windows 95® Version

You are about to begin a learning experience that many believe is an extremely important model for education in the future--the use of a simulation to learn a complex task. Simulations have been used for years to train airplane pilots and air traffic controllers, radar crews, submarine commanders, and more recently the crews of space vehicles.

There are a number of advantages to using simulations to enhance learning. One is that a highly complex situation can be tailored to the needs of the learner. Another is that time can be compressed or expanded to enhance the player's learning experience. A third advantage is that events which occur rarely in the real world can be simulated on demand.

The Business Strategy and Policy Game (BUSPOG) is a computer-based simulation of a real company. It is carefully crafted for students finishing their undergraduate business courses in order to challenge but not overwhelm them. It eliminates unnecessary details yet retains the complexity necessary to highlight the important concepts of managing a company. At the end of the game, learners have an understanding of not only their company's major functions but also the company's relationship to its industry, its competitors, and its environment.

This business simulation provides an ideal environment for integrating business concepts gained in specialized classes; e.g., accounting, marketing, quantitative methods. It elicits unusually high levels of energy, attention, and diligence. The result is players work harder, learn more, and seem to enjoy the experience.

The Business Strategy and Policy Game is not new. The first version of the game appeared in 1981, authored by David Eldredge and Don Bates. It was quickly implemented on a variety of computer systems in the United States and Canada and was translated into several other languages including Japanese. In 1985 it was considered one of the three best games available and the best for undergraduate students, but it ran on mainframe computers in an increasingly microcomputerized world. A DOS version was developed in 1993 but was only promoted to those campuses using the mainframe game. This Windows 95® Version of BUSPOG presents a number of changes to the original game making it even more flexible and realistic. It reorganizes and expands the original player's manual to support the use of modern spreadsheet programs (which many students claim doubles the learning). It presents new sections on the use of quantitative techniques, such as forecasting and seasonality, and on the possible uses of simulation by real-world companies.

Special thanks. We would like to express our appreciation to Jo Jane Marshall, our editor, and to Barbara Miller for their time, energy, and dedication to this player's manual. Without their loyal support the *Windows 95® Version of the Business Strategy and Policy Game* would still be a goal not a result.

Contents

Introduction

1

In The Business Strategy and Policy Game (BUSPOG) you and your team members become top management of a simulated company in a simulated industry which sells videocassette recorders to an unlimited market of customers.

The industry in which you manage your company can consist of up to seven other companies exactly like yours. They sell exactly the same product to exactly the same customers as you. In addition, when the game begins, the condition of their company (their number of sales in each of the three markets, their inventories, their cash, etc.) is exactly the same as yours. The only differences between the companies are the effects that will be seen following the decisions your team and the other teams make.

As top management in a BUSPOG company every quarter you will make a set of twenty decisions: five Marketing decisions, five Production decisions, five Human Resource decisions, and five decisions relating to Financial and Accounting variables. The size of your industry and whether your company gains or loses position relative to your competitors will depend on the effectiveness of your decisions.

At the beginning of each round of play, you will start from the position you had at the end of the last quarter. Depending on where you start, where your competitors start, their strategies, your strategy, and a number of industry variables, you will make and enter your set of twenty new decisions. Once decisions are available from each team, the game administrator will run the game and provide reports for each team.

These printed reports at the end of each quarter which result from running the game are the starting points for the next round of play.

At the beginning of the game you will probably base your **decisions** on principles you bring to the learning situation:

- It is good to cut costs as much as possible.
- It is wise to put some of the profit in a savings account for an emergency.
- Since the work-force is skillful enough, and $20,000 is a lot of money to spend on training, we should cut training.

Similarly you will base your **interpretation of results** on principles you bring to the game:

- It is important to make a profit every quarter.
- Profit is more important than market share.
- We should always have the highest possible stock price, etc.

Hold on to the principles you bring to the game as long as they get the results you want, but be sure to check the results. In most cases in BUSPOG response to actions are about the same as in the real world. When you don't get the results you expect, go back to your sources of information (such as textbooks) to see if you have remembered the principles correctly. Talk to previous instructors and your game administrator about which actions achieve what results. (Sometimes these are called cause-effect relationships.) Above all else, read and re-read the chapters in this BUSPOG player's manual whenever you are looking for concepts which make more sense.

The player's manual is organized so that the parts you need first come first. More complex information is presented later when you are better able to understand it.

Before making your first set of decisions, you should be familiar with Chapters 1 through 5. Chapter 6 will make more sense after you have gained some experience with the Business Strategy and Policy game. In Chapter 6 there is a review of the principles of managerial planning, implementing, and controlling. It is important to know what you are trying to achieve, to have goals and objectives. If you don't know where you are going, any road will do.

Chapters 7 through 10 provide detailed information about each of the Functional Specialties, including the formulas BUSPOG uses to calculate the responses to your decisions. As you become familiar with these formulas, you will increasingly base your decisions on them -- tempered by judgment, of course. As you use more and more of them, you will probably recognize they require too much time to use hand calculations. At this point we suggest you begin to build a spreadsheet to facilitate these calculations.

Chapter 11 is focused on how to build a spreadsheet to support your decision-making. (Information systems specialists call this a Decision Support System.) If you build it well enough, you will know the results of your decisions before the game is run.

In Chapters 12 is a discussion of quantitative techniques which you may want to use as you gain more experience with the game and want to perfect your managerial skill. Here we demonstrate the use of graphs, ratios, and more complex calculations.

If you build a fully integrated spreadsheet, you will experience how a well-functioning decision support system makes management in BUSPOG easier and more effective. In Chapter 13 we build upon this experience to demonstrate some of the ways real-world companies use simulation to improve their results and clarify the dynamics in which they manage.

Finally, in Chapter 14, we summarize the BUSPOG learning experience including:
- all parts of a business are interconnected
- problems determine which are the most important parts of an organization
- decisions must have objective support.
- preparing for the unexpected provides a valuable edge
- the only way to determine which cause-effect relationships should be used is to compare predictions with results.

This final summary is crucial to consolidating the insights you will gained as you play The Business Strategy and Policy Game

Game Description

2

You and your team members have just been hired to become the Top Management Team of a simulated company in a simulated industry which sells videocassette recorders to an unlimited market of customers.

Your company has been doing business for a number of years, but for some reason they have not shared with you, they summarily fired their previous Top Management Team and chose you.

The Industry

An industry is a group of companies which sell similar products to the same customers. Your industry will be made up of as many as seven companies. All of the companies are in the business of selling videocassette recorders to the same customers. In addition, all of the companies have the same organizational structure: Marketing, Production, Finance/Accounting, and Human Resources.

At the beginning of the game all of the companies in the industry start at the same point. Last quarter (Year 2, Quarter 4) you set the same price for your product in each market, you sold the same number of recorders in each market, you had the same number of production workers. In short, your competitors start from the same place you do. While this may not be realistic, it is a simple and effective way to compare the performance of your company with the performance of your competitors.

The companies will not stay the same because every quarter the management team of each company will make a new set of 20 decisions. As a result, some companies will move ahead, and some will fall back.

The BUSPOG computer program incorporates a number of hypothetical relationships in your industry. Some of these hypothetical relationships relate the companies to the economic environment of the industry; others relate the companies to each other. These relationships represent a conceptualization or model of the ways such an industry and its environment might behave. Although the model was developed with a concern for realism, it is a considerable simplification of the real world.

Some relationships in the real world are known with a high degree of certainty while others are only vaguely known. For example, the cost of production is quite predictable for most manufacturing operations, but the connection between level of advertising and demand for your product is significantly less predictable; the same is true for most of the other marketing activities. This is also the situation in BUSPOG. Some of the relationships are quite specific, while others are represented in fairly general terms.

The Individual Company

The total operations for an individual BUSPOG company are shown in Figure 2-1. This conceptualization does not show all the relationships and elements in the company's operations, but it does

Figure 2-1
Overall Organizational Operations

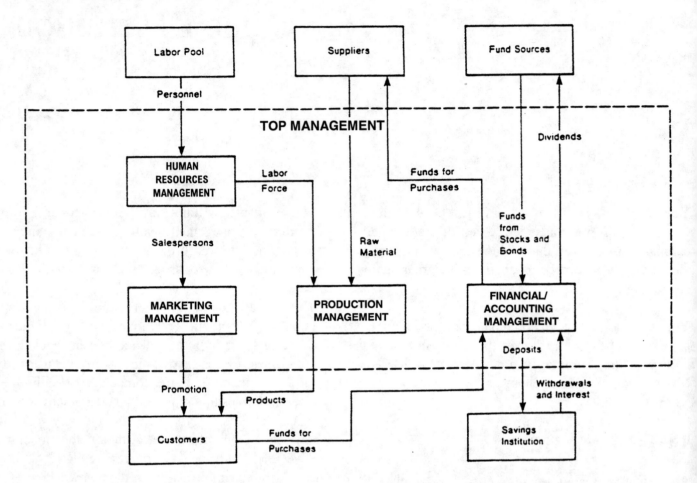

depict the major ones. As indicated in the figure, Top Management is not only concerned with the company's internal operations but also with the company's interfaces with its external environment.

Internal Operations

Each BUSPOG team manages a hypothetical company that has been in existence for a number of years. (The historical data for each company for the last two years are presented in Appendix A.)

You have two types of customers. Retail customers buy most of your videocassette recorders, but industrial customers also buy a significant number. Your previous marketing manager organized your marketing activity into one segment focusing on retail sales and another segment focusing on industrial sales. In addition, because the retail segment is so

large (and may not respond in the same way to a single sales program), the retail market has been divided into two geographical areas. To be precise, Market 1 (the first retail market) is the area east of the Mississippi River, Market 2 (the second retail market) is the area west of the Mississippi River. Market 3 includes all of the industrial customers. Each market has its own warehouse which receives Finished Product from the factory and stores the product until it is delivered to customers.

All of your videocassette recorders are manufactured in a single production facility and are then shipped to the warehouses. The number of units transported to any particular market is determined by an Allocation figure which is the percentage of the Total Production each market should receive. Once a unit of Finished Product is shipped to a warehouse, it stays in that warehouse until sold. This manufacturing-distribution system is shown in Figure 2-2

4

Figure 2-2
Manufacturing-Distribution System

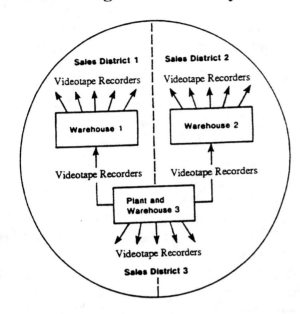

Let us focus now on your **Marketing** activity. Each of your markets has its own Sales Force. Every person in this Sales Force is equally effective (each one sells the same number of units). When you want to increase the number of Salespeople in a market, you must hire Sales Trainees. One quarter after you hire trainees, they join your Sales Force.

The number of sales per Salesperson is an indication of the effectiveness of your Sales Force. There are three ways to improve the effectiveness of your Sales Force:
1. Make your product easier to sell.
2. Make your Sales Force more skillful.
3. Increase the motivation of your Salespeople.

Investment in Product R&D makes the product easier to sell (e.g., makes it work better, makes it look better, makes it easier to maintain, etc.). Investment in Sales Training makes your Salespeople more skillful. Increasing the Sales Commissions and/or increasing Profit-Sharing increases the motivation of your Sales force to accomplish more.

Focusing on the function of **Production** you must determine the number of units you need to produce in a quarter. It is the sum of the number of new units required in each of these Markets. The number of finished videocassette recorders required in each

market is determined by considering the number you start with, the number you expect to sell in that market, and the number you want to have in inventory at the end of the quarter.

The number of units that can be produced in any particular quarter is a function of (the number of people in your production Workforce) times (the number of hours they work during the quarter) times the number of units they produce in one production hour-- their Productivity.

Productivity is a function of three factors in both the real world and BUSPOG:
1. The technology used in your production process.
2. The skill of your Production Workers.
3. The motivation of your Production Workers

Production technology is improved by investments in Process Research and Development; in this activity new technology is developed and new equipment and technology are installed. Production skills are improved by investments in Production Training. To improve motivation of Production Workers increase investments in Profit-Sharing.

Forty hours is a normal workweek for which Production Workers receive their usual wage per hour times 40. You can ask your workers to work up to 60 hours per week, but the overtime hours cost time and a half (the usual wage rate times 1.5). If you ask Production Workers to work less than 40 hours per week, you will still pay them for 40 hours because that was set in the contract negotiated by their labor union.

External Environment

The External Environment in the real world is everything that is outside the boundaries of the company. Because this External Environment is so complex, it is usually divided into the Task Environment (customers, competitors, suppliers, and other elements that relate to the task of the company) and the Broad Environment (everything else such as the "socio-cultural, political, legal, and economic factors). . In BUSPOG only the economic aspects for the Broad Environment are considered.

Task Environment

The Task Environment includes all of the aspects of the External Environment that relate to the primary task of the company: the suppliers with whom the company interacts to obtain the resources (labor, raw material , finances) their operations require customers and competitors.

Figure 2-1 presents the Task Environment of each company in your BUSPOG industry.

All of the teams in your industry are competing for Sales to an unlimited pool of customers. The Market Share of each competing company depends entirely on the decisions of each company's Top Management Team.

Similarly, there is an unlimited labor pool from which you can hire both Production Workers and Sales-people. If you decide to hire 5,000 Production Workers you will get them. In BUSPOG, this labor pool is so large you need not worry about workers taking your strategy or technology to competitors if you decide to fire them. In the real world this is not always true

If you were making videocassette recorders in the real world, you would have to maintain Receiving Goods Inventories for perhaps two hundred different parts and subassemblies. Managing two hundred inventories is just two hundred times the work of managing one. In BUSPOG you must manage only one type of Receiving Inventory which is called Raw Material. All the Raw Material you need for your production process comes from one supplier and, as in all monopoly situations, you have no recourse to the supplier's decisions on price. If you need raw material in any particular quarter, you must pay the price quoted. Fortunately, the same price is quoted to your competitors.

Also, this supplier is so big you can be assured you will receive any amount of raw material you order. For example, if you need five hundred million pounds of Raw Material, you will receive your shipment on the date expected.

Unfortunately, in monopoly situations the supplier is not very customer-oriented. You will not receive your Raw Material until the end of the quarter for which you place your order, too late for use in the quarter. For this reason, you must anticipate production needs for the following quarter when placing an order for Raw Material in the current quarter. If you run out of raw material before the end of the quarter, your Production Workforce will sit around until next quarter, producing nothing for the pay which you give them.

Decisions for the Financial/Accounting function are easier in some ways in BUSPOG and more difficult in others. Should waht you want to do costs more than you can obtain from internal sources, you can use either Debt Financing or Equity financing. Deciding which of two kinds of debt financing to use will depend on the length of time you anticipate needing the money. If you need short-term financing, you can request a Bank Loan from your banker. This loan will come due in ninety days, and your banker will take the principal (and the interest due) directly from your Cash Account. If you request a Bank Loan, you will get it, and taking the loan will not necessarily increase your loan interest rate.

If you want to use Debt Financing for a longer period of time, you can sell Bonds. If you offer to sell a Bond, someone will buy it. For simplicity, in BUSPOG unlike in the real world Bonds are more like long-term-variable interest loans. Once sold, they never come due during the game, but you must service the debt each quarter by paying the appropriate interest: (Bonds Outstanding) times one-fourth (the Current Bond Interest Rate). When you have surplus Cash, you can call back the Bonds, but you must pay a six percent Call Premium.

You can also finance long- term investments by selling Equity such as Shares of Stock. If you offer to sell stock, someone will buy it at the price quoted in your last printout or Output Report. As in the real world, you never have to pay interest on funds raised by selling equity. But in the game, once you sell stock, you can never get it back.

The good news is you can always receive credit in BUSPOG. Somebody will always accommodate you if you decide to use either debt or equity financing. The bad news is -- as your industry recognizes the condition of your financial performance and your inability to manage it, your Interest Rates will be raised. While quoted Interest Rates are for the year, actual charges are for one quarter at a time.

Another aspect of your Financial/Accounting environment is the savings institution. Skilled financial managers add significantly to the profit of the company by earning interest on all spare Cash. In BUSPOG, when there is no better investment opportunity, the investment of unneeded Cash with a savings institution is a significant source of profit. The Annual Interest Rate for all money in your savings account is eight percent.

Your competitors are the final aspect of the Task Environment , and there is no way to know before the game begins what your competitors are going to do. Perhaps they will be highly passive or highly aggressive. Perhaps they will be uninformed (or stupid). Remember, your competitors start where you do, and you can learn a lot about them by watching what they do and by listening to what they say. It will be in your interest to pick up the Sales they cannot deliver because they have run out of Finished Product Inventory. Listen carefully for information indicating they are likely to Stock Out and increase your own Finished Product Inventory when such a thing seems possible.

Broad Environment: Economic Aspects

The simulated Economic Environment of BUSPOG is quite similar to that of the real world since it considers these six variables:

1. Gross Domestic Product
2. Personal Consumption Expenditures for Durable Goods
3. Number of Household Formations
4. Bond Interest Rate
5. Loan Interest Rate
6. Raw Material Cost

Historical values for these six variables are given in Appendix A. In addition, current values are reported each quarter in **Economy and Stock Market** (Section 5 of the Output Report)

The first three economic variables are considered Coincident Economic Indicators in the game. They forecast the level of economic activity for the current quarter. In the real world the demand for a durable product, such as a videotape recorder, is related to the current level of economic activity. This is also true in the Business Strategy and Policy Game. It can be hypothesized that the Product Demand in BUSPOG is directly related to the levels of the Gross Domestic Product, Personal Consumption Expenditures for Durable Goods, and the Number of Household Formations. When these variables go up, Demand will probably go up.

The level of the effects of these factors on Product Demand can be estimated from the historical data in Appendix A through an eyeball approach or a statistical process such as Regression Analysis. Should the Top Management Team of a company determine the effect of one or more of these indices is negligible in comparison to the effect of other variables, it can be ignored. Regardless of a team's approach, the estimate of the effect of these and any other variables in the game can be refined as the competition progresses and as more data become available.

The remaining three economic variables of Bond Interest Rate, Loan Interest Rate, and Raw Material Cost are leading economic indicators. These tend to shift direction prior to a change in the general level of economic activity. As such, they may be helpful in forecasting values for the Coincident Economic Indicators or for future Product Demand. Forecasts of values for these three variables are helpful in predicting future values affecting the financial status of a company. In particular, forecasts of Bond and Loan Interest Rates facilitate an estimate of the cost of Debt Capital. A forecast of the Cost of Raw Material provides a major input into an estimate of Production Costs.

Making Your First Decisions

3

The Business Strategy and Policy Game can be played at two different levels: by learners who are just beginning to study the complex world of business and by learners who are completing their introductory courses in the various subdivisions of the subject. These introductory courses have supplied a great deal of information, but they must be integrated into the kind of meaningful whole found in a real company.

Both those just beginning their study of business and those with an unintegrated understanding of each area will probably begin making **decisions** in the same way -- following their intuition based on what they think the situation should be. Both groups of learners will probably **interpret their first results** based on intuition and in relation to the results of their competitors.

Shortly after beginning to play the game, the more advanced learners will begin to bring in concepts they have learned in their courses -- concepts like safety stock (BUSPOG calls it Finished Product Inventories), the degree of elasticity in the demand curve, break-even points, market share, productivity, etc.

Success in playing The Business Strategy and Policy Game has very little to do with luck or guessing. Like managing a business in the real world, managing a BUSPOG company is largely a matter of dedication, hard work, understanding the situation, and the application of proved principles.

The Fundamentals

The Top Management Team of each BUSPOG company makes a number of decisions each quarter which are expected to help the team achieve their goals, in conformance with the policies they have adopted.

Three essential aspects in making a good decision are:
1. There is more than one acceptable alternative choice.
2. Future outcomes or results are somewhat uncertain.
3. There is a goal to be accomplished.

Management decisions are based on intuition or analysis or a combination of the two. Some decisions are based on intuition only. Most are based on intuition plus analysis. A few are based on analysis alone.

An analytical technique, by merely providing a structure for a situation, will make the best choice intuitively obvious to the decision-maker. Analytical techniques will support the decision-maker in reducing the size and complexity of the situation by summarizing major parts (e.g., calculating ratios or measures of central tendency and/or scatter).

Decision-Making Procedure

Analytic frameworks for aiding intuition-based decisions of the Top Management Team are provided in Chapters 6 through 10 of this text. Unfortunately, this procedure requires an investment of time and an application of information by the management team which may not be possible at the beginning of the game. As play progresses, however, it should be increasingly utilized. The improved result will provide a better learning experience in terms of both developing good managerial skills and handling the game's competitive aspects.

When you are faced with an overly-short preparation time or when the complexity of the information seems overwhelming, return to this chapter for a simplified approach to making a set of decisions and for a summary of the major steps in the procedures provided in Chapters 6 through 10.

Successful Decision-Making

All decision-making procedures in BUSPOG, whether they rely on analysis plus intuition or intuition alone, must result in decisions that ensure the company will not run out of:

- Finished Products
- Raw Material
- Cash.

If a company runs out of Finished Products, it will lose sales and customers, and give a free boost to competitors. Obviously, this stock out leads to a poor financial performance. If a company has insufficient Raw Material, it cannot produce all the Finished Products planned, and a stock out may occur. In addition, since the Production Work- force is paid for forty hours per week whether the plant is producing or not, a nonproductive plant further drains the company's financial resources. If a company runs out of Cash, it is viewed as a poor risk by creditors. This results in a substantial increase in the Loan and Bond Interest Rates furthering weakening the company's financial position.

The most important safeguard in avoiding the depletion of Finished Product, Raw Material, and Cash resources is the forecast of Demand. An accurate forecast of demand provides the basis for determining how much Finished Product to manufacture and how to distribute it to each of the three markets. The estimate of Demand for the next decision period also provides the basis for determining how much Raw Material to order this period for next period's Production. Finally, the Forecast Demand provides the basis for determining whether the funds available exceed or at least match the funds needed by the company.

In summary, successful BUSPOG decision making involves at the minimum four elements:
1. a Sales Forecast for each of the three markets for the next two quarters
2. a Production Plan for the next quarter
3. a Raw Material Plan for the next quarter
4. a Cash Budget for the next quarter

Time and again it has been proven that those participants who have the greatest success, in BUSPOG competition and in learning through the BUSPOG experience, base their decisions on these four elements plus other criteria. To attain any success at all these four plans must be completed, at first perhaps, by hand, but, later, by using well-developed spreadsheets.

Back to Reality

Whether you lack sufficient time to understand what all this means or there is just too much information, you may be feeling overwhelmed. What can you do now to combine the theory you know and the data provided in the game manual to make your first set of decisions?

Review What You Know

As you prepare to enter your first decisions in the BUSPOG game there are several things you may do. First, review what you know about the principles of business.

What do you know about **Marketing**? How can you determine whether you should raise or lower Prices? What percentage of Gross Sales should you spend on Advertising? How can you determine the absolute and relative effectiveness of your Sales Force? How can you improve the effectiveness of your Sales Force? How can you forecast the number of units your customers will buy next quarter and the quarter after that?

What do you know about **Production**? How large should your Receiving Goods Inventories be? Your Finished Product Inventories? Considering the state of your Finished Product Inventories and the anticipated Demand for your product next quarter, how many units should you make? How large a Production Work Force should you maintain? How can you determine the absolute and relative effectiveness of your Production Work Force? How can you enhance it?

What do you know about **Human Resources**? How much should you pay your Salespeople and your Production Workers? What factors would indicate if you are not paying enough? How can you enhance the energy and attention your work-force puts into their work? How much should you spend on Research and Development? The other side of Human Resources concerns the effectiveness of your BUSPOG team: Are all the members of your team participating actively in discussions? Are they informed or are they just guessing? Whose comments turn out to be correct? Are they doing their homework?

What do you know about **Finance and Accounting**? What factors indicate you need additional financing? Should you use Debt or Equity Financing? How much profit did you make last quarter and how much is your company worth? How much should you ask for your Product?

Study the History

A second step in preparing to make your first set of decisions is to understand how your company has been doing. In Appendix A of the player's manual you will find a series of eight BUSPOG reports. In the upper right hand corner of the first report you will see it is reporting the results of the set of decisions made for Year 1, Quarter 1. Turn to the next page. It is for Year 1, Quarter 2. The next is for Quarter 3, and so forth until the last one reports the results for Year 2, Quarter 4. This series of eight reports gives the history for every company in your industry for the last two years (as noted previously, in the beginning all the companies teams have the same history). Study this history carefully. You may be able to identify both effective and ineffective practices of previous management. Is the total market for videocassette recorders growing? How fast? What is happening to your company's Market Share? Are there trends in Pricing? Advertising? Productivity? Purchasing Raw Material? Is there seasonality in Demand? How much? Do you see a change in the performance of the company either internally or in relation to the previous competitors?

Check Present Position

The third step when preparing to make your first set of decisions is to study carefully the report for Year 2, Quarter 4 in Appendix A. This report gives the position from which each team begins making decisions. From this report you can determine how much Cash you have in your Cash Account, how many people you have in your Production Work Force, the levels of your Inventories, etc. Are there imbalances and inconsistencies that need to be rectified?

Management Decisions

The simulated competition of BUSPOG requires that the Top Management Team for each company make a set of decisions for each quarter of each year of play. The particular decisions which must be made each decision period include:

Marketing
1. Selling Price in each of the Three Markets
2. Advertising Budget for each of the Three Markets
3. Salespersons to be hired or discharged in each of the Three Markets
4. Investment to be made in Product Research and Development
5. Sales Commission to be paid

Production
1. Production Workweek scheduled
2. Change to be made in the Production Workforce
3. Allocation of Finished Product to each of the Three Markets
4. Investment to be made in Process Research and Development
5. Raw Materials to be ordered

Human Resources
1. Sales Salaries
2. Sales Training Budget
3. Production Wage rate
4. Production training Budget
5. Profit Sharing

Finance
1. Bonds to be sold or redeemed
2. Bank Loan to be requested
3. Dividends to be paid
4. Stock to be issued
5. Deposit to or withdrawal from the Savings Account

Making your first decisions may be especially daunting because you may have no idea what effect your decisions will have. While some game administrators will give more information than others, the only way to identify the relationship between a particular action and its effects is to try it and observe what happens.

Management decisions are always based on a combination of both objective data and subjective feelings. In the beginning of the BUSPOG experience, most decisions will be based on subjective judgment. With experience and learning, however, most of this guessing will be left behind; decisions will be based primarily on calculations. The sooner you understand the internal relationships, the sooner the outcomes will become predictable, the better will be the results of your company's operations, and the more enjoyable will be your learning experience.

Perhaps the most important learning which can occur from any capstone learning experience is discovering ways to identify the **cause-effect relations** which underlie the practice of management in real companies and to identify when these relationships change. In order to provide an opportunity for you to learn what will happen when you change the previous management's decisions, the game usually starts with one or more trials. At the end of these trials the game is reset to its beginning point, and you start playing for the record.

These trials have a dual purpose. First, you become familiar with the details of the game: the units of each decision, how you enter decisions, what your Output Reports mean. Another, equally important purpose of these trials is to provide an opportunity to learn the effects that result from the changes you make. Do not be afraid to make what you may consider stupid decisions; the results of these trials are off the record. What matters in the trials is that you begin to learn the cause-effect relationships in the game.

Table 3-1
Decision Variable Summary

Decision Variable	Units of Measurement	Restrictions on Values	Value For Year 2, Quarter 4
Product Price	dollars	Min.: 0 Max.: 2000	$300 in each market
Advertising Budget	1000s of dollars	Min.: 0 Max.: 5000	$300,000 in each market
Sales Force Change	number of persons	Min.: minus number Max.: 500	Mkt. 1: +2 Mkt. 2: 0 Mkt. 3: +3
Product R&D Budget	1000s of dollars	Min.: 0 Max.: 30,000	$50,000
Sales Commission percentage		Min.: 0 Max.: 100%	0.4%
Production Work Week	hours per week	Min.: 0 Max.: 60	40 hours
Labor Force Change	number of persons	Min.: minus no. In force Max.: 5000	+400
Allocation of Finished Products	percentage	Min.: 0 Max.: 100 Sum of 3 =100%	Mkt.1: 43% Mkt.2: 37% Mkt. 3: 20%
Process R&D Budget	1000s of dollars	Min.: 0 Max.: 30,000	$40,000
Raw Material Ordered	Millions of Pounds	Min.: 0 Max.: 500	0
Sales Salary	dollars per month	Min.: 0 Max.: 100,000	$1.500
Sales Training Budget	1000s of dollars	Min.: 0 Max.: 30,000	$25,000
Production Wage Rate	dollars per hour	Min.: 0 Max.: 50	$5.50
Prod. Training Budget	1000s of dollars	Min.: 0 Max.: 30,000	$15,000
Profit Sharing	percentage	Min.: 0 Max.: 100	0.3%
Bonds Sold or Redeemed	1000s of dollars	Min.: minus bonds Max.:	0
Bank Loan Requested	1000s of dollars	Min.: 0 Max.: 30,000	0
Dividends Paid	1000s of dollars	Min.: 0 Max.: 30,000	$3,000,000
Stock Issued	1000s of shares	Min.: 0 Max.: 32,000	0
Savings Deposit or Withdrawal	1000s of dollars	Min.: minus acct. bal. Max.:	$1,500,000

You will notice that some of the numbers in the history and on the decision sheets are presented in different types of units. If at first this seems confusing, be assured this confusion goes away after a few rounds of play. Such factors as Unit Sales, Production Workers, Sales People, and Production Hours per Week, are presented in units. Most financial data is presented in thousands of dollars (which requires you to add three zeros to convert numbers to dollars). Profit Sharing, Sales Commission, and Allocation of Finished Production to the Three Markets are reported as percentages. Raw Material is in millions of pounds (which requires you to add six zeros). In every case, these units are indicated on the Output Report and on the Quarterly Decision Sheets presented in Appendix B. These units of measure are summarized in **Table 3-1.** It is important to become familiar with the units in this report structure as soon as possible in order to avoid serious errors which can create problems with the game.

To demonstrate how important it is to pay attention to these units of measure, suppose you decide to order thirty million pounds of Raw Material and the Price quoted is $.49 a pound. Checking with your calculator you anticipate an extra charge of $9,800,000. Your Vice-president of Finance does not think you will have that much extra Cash. You then decide to request a bank loan of $10,000,000 to pay for it. If you enter $10,000,000 on your Decision Sheet (not realizing that bank loans are in thousands of dollars), you will get $10,000,000,000. Now ten billion dollars in your cash account may be great this quarter, but the bank will take that much out of your Cash Account next quarter (probably causing you to take an Emergency Loan, which will increase your Loan Interest Rate considerably). In addition, you will have to pay interest on that loan. If your interest rate is 13% annually, that mistake will cost you $324,675,000. You can see the point -- the importance of paying attention to the size of the units in which your decisions are registered.

Figure 3-1
Growth Curve Relationship

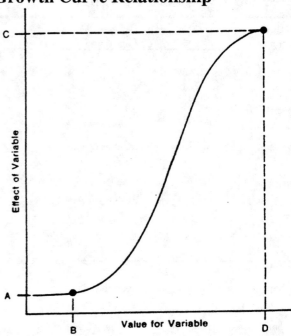

The general relationship of many of the variables in BUSPOG takes the form of what is termed a growth curve as shown in Figure 3-1. The growth curve relationship has a minimum effect level, which is "A" in Figure 3-1. If the value of your decision for the variable is at a level of "B" or less, the effect of the variable is at the minimum level "A". As your decision to change the value of the variable becomes larger than "B", the effect of the change increases according to the growth curve until a maximum effect of "C" is reached by a decision of "D". If investments become greater than "D", the effect of the variable remains unchanged at its maximum value "C".

To summarize, low levels of investment have very little effect. There is a minimum threshold value of most variables which is necessary in order to increase the effect. After the threshold value has been achieved, an increase in the variable has an increased effect until a maximum effect is attained. Increases in the variable above the saturation value are wasted since no corresponding increased effect is achieved. It is very important that the "B" and the "D" points are determined during the trial period.

In addition, the relationships depicted by the Growth Curve Model (Figure 3-1) may be felt in more than one time period. For example, the effect of expenditures on Advertising made during a particular quarter of the year may not only influence the product demand in that quarter but also in the next quarter and perhaps in later quarters. This lag in response is more pronounced for some variables than for others.

One point should be made before we proceed with a discussion of decision making in specific functional areas. Problems frequently occur in both the real world and also in BUSPOG when it is assumed that once one person assumes responsibility for a functional area, that person also has the right to make decisions in that area unilaterally. While you can adopt this as a policy for your company (especially in the beginning of the game), there is no guarantee this approach will achieve the best results. As a general rule, functional specialists should be prepared to recommend and defend decisions in their area of responsibility at the beginning of a session but the whole management team should concur on the final decision.

Marketing Decisions

Marketing is the part of most real-world industrial organizations that is primarily concerned with a company's customers. The marketing function in BUSPOG is also the primary informational link with your customers. In the game, this link is created through five decisions:

1. Selling Price in each of the three markets
2. Advertising Budget for each of the Three Markets
3. Salespersons to be hired or discharged in each of the Three Markets
4. Investment to be made in Product Research and Development
5. Sales Commissions to be paid

One of the most important marketing decisions in this game is choosing the Selling Price for each market.

Should you raise your price, lower it, or leave it alone?

"It all depends--" Students invariably say,

"On what?"

"On which makes the most profit."

Everyone seems to know that if you reduce the price of a product the amount you sell will go up. Similarly, if you raise the price, the amount you sell will go down.

With a little encouragement most students also come to recognize that if you reduce price, you reduce the profit which comes from each sale (the difference between the cost to make a product and its price). Similarly, if you increase price, the contribution to profit of each unit sold goes up.

If the number of Sales go up enough as you decrease your price, you make more by reducing the price. If they don't go up enough, you make less by lowering your price. Should you raise or lower prices? It depends on the characteristics of your Demand Curve. If the curve is sufficiently elastic (demand goes up as price is reduced), you should lower your price.

What is the elasticity in demand in BUSPOG? Reduce price (or increase it) and watch what happens to the profit. If profit goes up, reduce price (or increase it) again and again until the relationship between price and profit, (in this situation), is understood.

On the second decision, ask, "Which is more profitable, increasing investments in Advertising or lowering price?" Again, try it and evaluate the results. While we can't be certain the answers themselves can be transferred to the real world, the process certainly can.

Production has an index of effectiveness called Productivity which is actually the units produced in each production hour. Although it is not as obvious, there is a similar index of effectiveness for your Sales Force which can be calculated by

15

dividing sales by the number of salespeople in each market. Productivity is reported on the printout. Sales per salesperson must be calculated. Effectiveness of your sales force can be increased by improving the technology of your product (to make your product look or work better), improving the skill of your Sales Force, and by improving the motivation of your Sales Force. The technology of your product can be improved by investments in Product Research and Development, the skill of your Sales Force can be improved by investments in sales training, and the motivation of your Sales Force can be improved by increasing the sales commission.

The effect on demand of the five Marketing decisions concerning (1) Sales Price levels, (2) Advertising Expenditures, (3) Sales Force size of the levels (4) expenditures on Product Research and Development, and (5) levels of Sales Commissions has the Growth Curve relationships described in the discussion of Figure 3-1 and the lagged response.

In addition, Demand for your product is partially determined by variables within the Economic Environment, the Human Resources function, and the underlying demand pattern as a function of time (trending, seasonal, cyclic, and/or irregular in nature).

Based on all these considerations, the Marketing Vice President forecasts the number of sales in each market which may or may not be modified by other members of the Top Management Team. The Sales Forecast is critical to the success of a BUSPOG team because these projections serve as the basis for planning all the other activities of the organization. If you know your level of Sales, you can balance your Production, your Work Force, and your Finances.

Production Decisions

Production is that portion of the organization depicted in Figure 2-1 that is concerned with transforming Raw Materials and the efforts of the Production Workforce into Finished Products.

The number of units of Finished Products and their distribution to the Three Markets should be based on the Sales Forecast provided by Marketing and on policy for Ending Finished Product Inventories adopted by your Top Management Team.

On the other side of the equation, Production level is restricted by the number of Production Workers, the capacity of your plant and equipment, and the amount of raw material available.

In BUSPOG production decisions are next to the easiest area to calculate. Before the end of the trial period you should begin hand calculation of both the Production Plan and the Raw Material Requirements Plan, but even here subjective decisions will be requied.

The scheduled Production Work Week, change in the Production Labor Force, and Allocation of Finished Product to the Three Markets are all calculated on the Production Plan form and Raw Materials to order are calculated on the Raw Materials Plan form.

In BUSPOG as in the real world, productivity is the key to making a profit. The higher your Productivity, the less it costs you to make a finished videocassette recorder. The less it costs you to make a finished unit, the higher the spread between Cost and Selling Price and the greater your ability to compete with your competitors on price.

Three factors determine your level of Productivity: the relative quality of your production Technology, the skill of your production workers, and the motivation of your production work force. Technology is enhanced by investments in Process Research and Development. Skill is built by investments in Production Training. Motivation is built by investments in Profit Sharing. All three investments are controlled by the growth curve (Fig. 3-1) and lagged response.

Human Resources Decisions

Human Resources decisions, especially at first, are without doubt the easiest to make,. Sales Salaries and Production Wages are generally set in relation to the levels of your competitors and determined by your Wage and Salary Policy. According to various theories on motivation, if you pay less than the industry average, your employees will become dissatisfied and tend to voluntarily quit. If you pay more, they are not necessarily more motivated.

To repeat, investments in Sales Training increase the selling skill of your Salesforce, and investments in Production Training increase the skills of your Production Workforce. Investments in Profit Sharing increase the motivation of all your Work- force. All three are variables of the growth-curve, lagged response variables.

Financial/Accounting Decisions

The Chief Financial Officer (CFO) is responsible for the overall operation of all long-term and short-term financial and accounting operations of the firm. The person filling this position, therefore, must be competent and prepared to recommend a course of action through which the long-term and short-term goals of the organization can be achieved.

The biggest concern of the Chief Financial Officer when first making financial decisions is that there is enough Cash in your bank account to pay for all of the expenditures which you have authorized. In the real world, a CFO may arrange lines of credit with bankers. Lines of credit are like prearranged loans which are executed only when needed "(such as when the company does not earn enough Cash to pay for all their expenditures)." In BUSPOG an unlimited line of credit has been arranged to allow your banker to cover your checks whether or not their is a positive balance in your cash account. All loans, of course, earn interest from the time they are made.

Contrary to popular belief, bankers do not look down on people who take loans. In fact, bankers love to make loans, because that is the way they make money. What bankers do not like is when people who take loans but do not pay the interest required to service the debt and do not pay back the principal when it is due. In every situation involving a loan, there is always a risk that the principal and interest will not be repaid. The higher the risk, the higher the rate of interest the banker requires. When you require an emergency loan (because you do not have enough cash to satisfy your obligations), you get your loan but your rate of interest increases significantly.

In the beginning, the Chief Financial Officer's primary responsibility is to make sure that your company has sufficient Cash (and is not forced to take out an ermergency loan). The easiest way to do this is to make a copy of the Flow of Funds Statement for Year 2, Quarter 4. While a paper and pencil copy is quite adequate, you will discover a spreadsheet copy is much easier to use. (Copies of all calculation forms and the Year 2 Quarter 4 output Reports are provided on the disk which accompanies this manual.) Any decisions you make in relation to Marketing, Production, or Human Resources will have an effect on your Financial Decisions. For example, if you decide to increase Advertising, your Marketing costs will go up. If you decide to hire 200 Production Workers, your Labor costs will go up and your Production Force Change Costs will go up because there are charges associated with hiring or firing Production Workers. How much? To find out, check the company's history.

When you increase or decrease expenses and income, adjust the entries in the Flow of Funds Statement.

As a word of caution, the most usual cause of problems with Cash Flow at the beginning of the game is when you order Raw Materials and do not increase the Total Production Cost . For example if you order 10 million pounds of raw material at a quoted price of $.46 a pound, you will be increasing your Total Production Cost by $4,600,000. This amount should be added to your

Figure 3-2
Decision-Making Procedure Summary

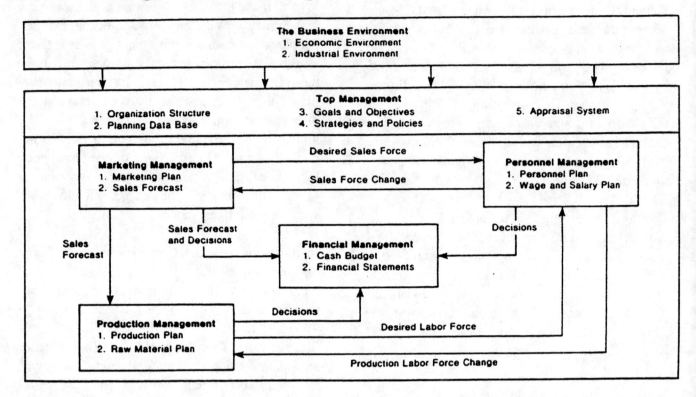

Total Production Cost on your Flow of Funds Statement .

More Sophisticated Decision-Making

Once you have made a round or two of decisions and evaluated the related results, you will probably want to begin increasing the sophistication of your decision making process. At this point it may help if you become familiar with Figure 3-2.

The analytic framework provided in Chapters 6 through 10 of this text requires an investment of time and application of information which most likely will not be available for several more rounds of play, but after a round or two begin to bring in more and more of these concepts and practices. Of course, the process should be increasingly utilized as play progresses since the improved result will provide a better learning experience.

A summary of the major steps in the procedures provided in Chapters 6 through 10 is presented next.

Managing Your Growth *(Chapter 6)*

1. *Organizational structure.* Establish the responsibilities of each member of the management team. In addition each team may select a name for its company.

2. *Planning data base.* Determine which variables of the many included in the output reports presented in Appendix A describe characteristics of your Industry, your Internal Situation, your Task Environment, and your Economic Environment that should be considered in your decisions.

3. *Mission, and Goals.* Define the long-range and short-range outcomes your organization wishes to achieve.

4. *Strategies, tactics, operations, and policies.* Develop the overall guiding philosophy into specific policies and select the shorter-range actions which will achieve the desired shorter-range result, in specific decision areas.

5. *Appraisal system.* Consider ways to interpret the results given in the output reports to determine the level of progress you have achieved toward your goals.

Marketing Management Considerations (Chapter 7)

1. *Marketing Plan.* Select values for all the marketing Decision Variables except the number of salespersons to be hired or discharged. For this number select the desired size of the Salesforce in each market and give these values to the Humann Resources Vice President who will determine the needed changes. Then forward the values for all five decisions to the Financial Vice President

2. *Sales Forecast.* Prepare a sales forecast for each of the three markets. Forward this to the Production and Financial Vice-Presidents.

Production Management Considerations (Chapter 8)

1. *Production Plan.* Select values for the scheduled **Production Work Week**, the **Production Force Required**, and the **Allocation of Finished Products** to the Three Markets. Give the value for the **Production Force Required** to the Human Resources Vice-President.

2. *Raw Materials Plan.* Select values for the **Raw Materials Ordered** and for the **Process Research & Development** Budget.

3. Forward values for these three decisions and the two above to the Financial Vice-President.

Human Resources Management Considerations (Chapter 9)

1. *Human Resources Plan.* Compute the required changes in the Sales Force and the Production Labor Force based on the desired levels. (You will probably want to ignore Voluntary Terminations at this point.) Forward values to the Marketing and Production Vice-Presidents

2.. *Wage and Salary plan.* Select values for the five Human Resources variables listed on the Quarterly Decision Sheet (Table 3-1). Forward values to the Financial Vice-President.

Financial Management Considerations (Chapter 10)

1. *Cash Budget Plan.* Estimate values for all the sources and uses of funds for the company. This requires estimating values for Production, Marketing, and Other costs on the *Cost Estimates Plan Form* (Table 10-2).

2. The *Income Statement* and the *Position Statement.* Since these statements are of little help at the beginning of play, they can be omitted for now.

Quarterly Decisions and Restrictions

Results are better and mistakes are fewer when values for the twenty quarterly decision variables are entered first on a **Decision Sheet** and then input into the game-disk.

Since an error on the **Decision Sheet** will result in an error in the decision variables (which will probably not achieve the results you want when they are input into the game), the Decision Sheet should be filled out carefully and correctly. Both data entries and computations should be cross-checked.

Table 3-2
Quarterly Decision Sheet

IDENTIFICATION

INDUSTRY   COMPANY   YEAR   QUARTER

_____   _____   _____   _____

MARKETING DECISIONS

PRODUCT PRICE (in dollars)   **ADVERTISING (thousands of $)**

MARKET 1   MARKET 2   MARKET 3   MARKET 1   MARKET 2   MARKET 3

_____ .   _____ .   _____ .   _____ .   _____ .   _____ .

SALES FORCE CHANGE (persons)   **PRODUCT R&D**   **SALES COMMISSION**

MARKET 1   MARKET 2   MARKET 3   (thousands $)   (percentage)

_____   _____   _____   _____ .   _____ . _

PRODUCTION DECISIONS

PRODUCTION WORK WEEK (hrs./week)	LABOR FORCE CHANGE (persons)	ALLOCATION OF FINISHED PROD. (percentage to each market)			PROCESS R&D ($1000)	RAW MATERIAL ORDERED (millions lbs.)
		MARKET 1	MARKET 2	MARKET 3		
_____ .	_____ .	_____ .	_____ .	_____ .	_____ .	_____ .

HUMAN RESOURCE DECISIONS

SALES SALARY SHARING (dollars/mo.)	SALES TRAINING (thousands $)	PRODUCTION WAGE (dollars/hr.)	PROD. TRAINING (thousands $)	PROFIT (percentage)
_____ .	_____ .	_____ .	_____ .	_____ . _

FINANCIAL DECISIONS

BONDS (thousands $)	BANK LOAN (thousands $)	DIVIDENDS PAID (thousands $)	STOCK ISSUED (1000s shares)	SAVINGS ACCOUNT (thousands $)
_____ .	_____ .	_____ .	_____ .	_____ .

An example of the **Quarterly Decision Sheet** is shown in **Table 3-2**. The sheet is divided into five sections:

1. Identification
2. Marketing Decisions
3. Production Decisions
4. Human Resource Decisions
5. Financial/Accounting Decisions

This format is used to enter your decisions on your student disk (before it is given to the game administrator) or into your student file if you are using a network. Additional Decision Sheets are in Appendix B.

Entering Your Decisions and Printing Your Results

4

Once you and your teammates agree on your first set of decisions and enter them on a Decision Sheet, it is time to create a computer disk on which your decisions will be submitted to your game administrator. (If your administrator is using a network, you will receive special instructions to fit your local situation.)

A computer disk accompanies your player's manual
usually inside a plastic envelope in the back of the book. As the game progresses, you will accumulate your decisions and your Output Report in a series of files on this disk. Included on this disk are all of the planning forms (discussed in other parts of the manual and in an EXCEL® 5.0 format) plus some strategic planning forms which may be of use.

First, remove the disk from your manual so it will be available. Since each member on your team has a disk, determine whose disk will be the master. Facilitate your work by entering all of your decisions on the selected disk. You can, of course, copy from this disk to other disks if you find it convenient.

Now start the computer on which you will enter your decisions. Once it boots up, select the BUSPOG program. (In most cases it will be available as a *shortcut*.)

The opening screen presents a picture similar to the one on the front of your player's manual. You are asked to **Put your data disk in Drive A: and click anywhere to continue**.

Once you do this, the BUSPOG Main Menu appears

Figure 4-1
Main Menu

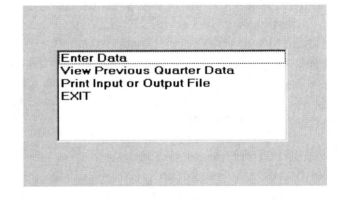

From this menu select **Enter Data**.

Now the Data Input screen appears with the Identification Data sheet in front.

Figure 4-2
Identification Data Input Menu

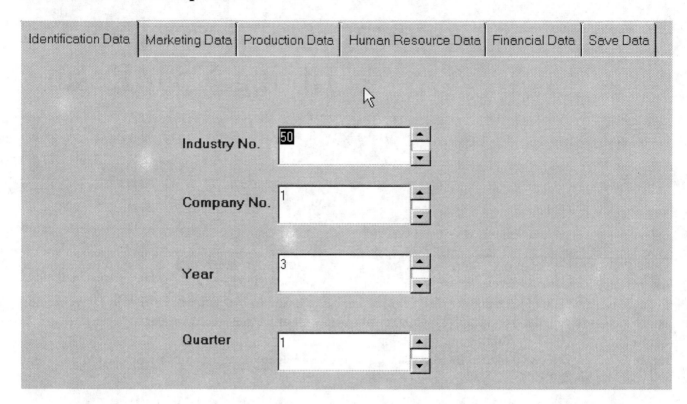

Enter the identification information from your **Quarterly Decision Sheet into the appropriate spaces**. Care should be taken to be sure this information is correct (especially the Industry and Company numbers). This is a safety feature of the program to prevent other companies putting their data into your files. In addition, each time the game administrator will check this information to be sure it is correct.

You can enter the appropriate data using your keyboard or the up and down arrows. In entering data from the keyboard, when ever the cursor square blinks blue, new data will replace what is presently in that window. To edit the entry you can use your mouse to place the cursor at any given position in the line of information in the window.

Press the Tab key to move to the next window.

While it may be obvious to most players, especially those who interact frequently with computers, it is not necessary to change every entry in a data sheet. If you an entry is correct, leave it alone.

Once you finish entering your Identification Data, click **Marketing Data**.

Figure 4-3
Marketing Data Menu

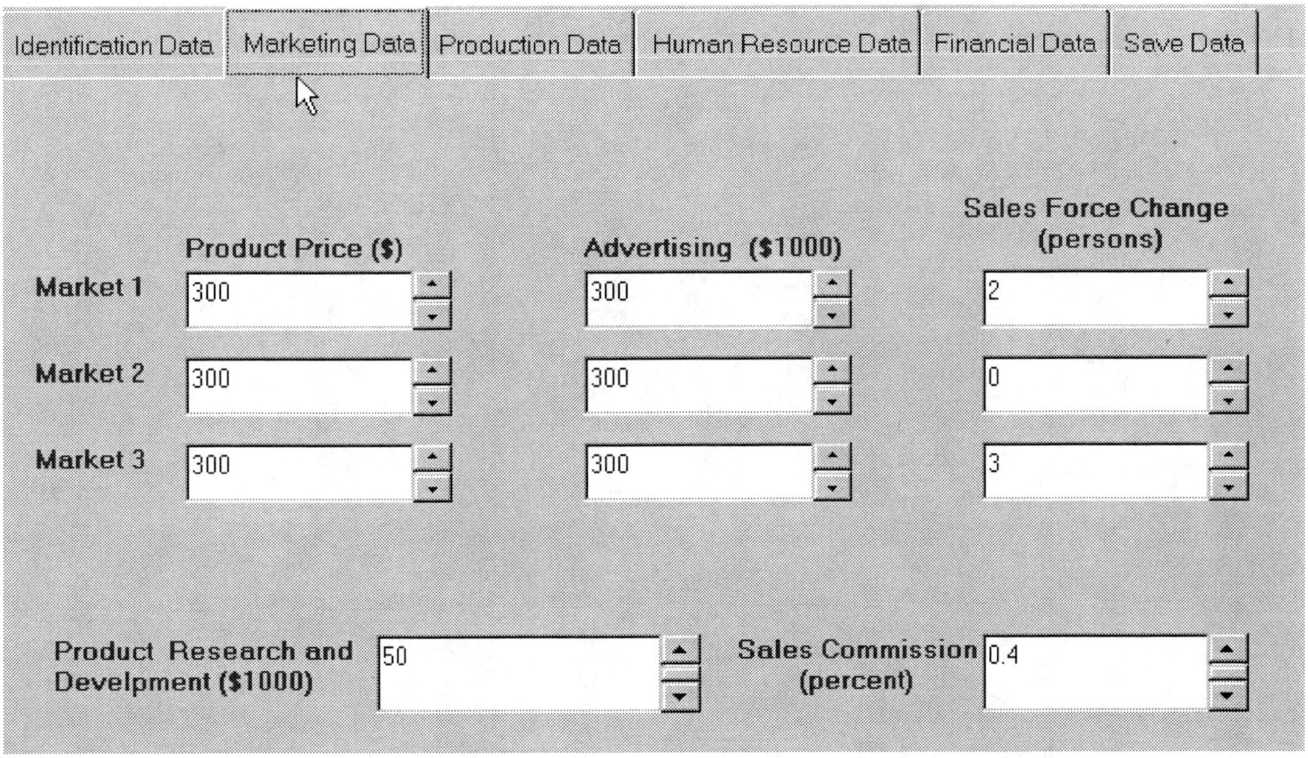

| Identification Data | Marketing Data | Production Data | Human Resource Data | Financial Data | Save Data |

	Product Price ($)	Advertising ($1000)	Sales Force Change (persons)
Market 1	300	300	2
Market 2	300	300	0
Market 3	300	300	3

| Product Research and Develpment ($1000) | 50 | Sales Commission (percent) | 0.4 |

Enter your Marketing Decisions in the appropriate windows and check them for accuracy. (To facilitate accuracy, have one person enter the data and another person check the accuracy of the entries.) When you finish, **click on Production Data.**

Figure 4-4
Production Data Menu

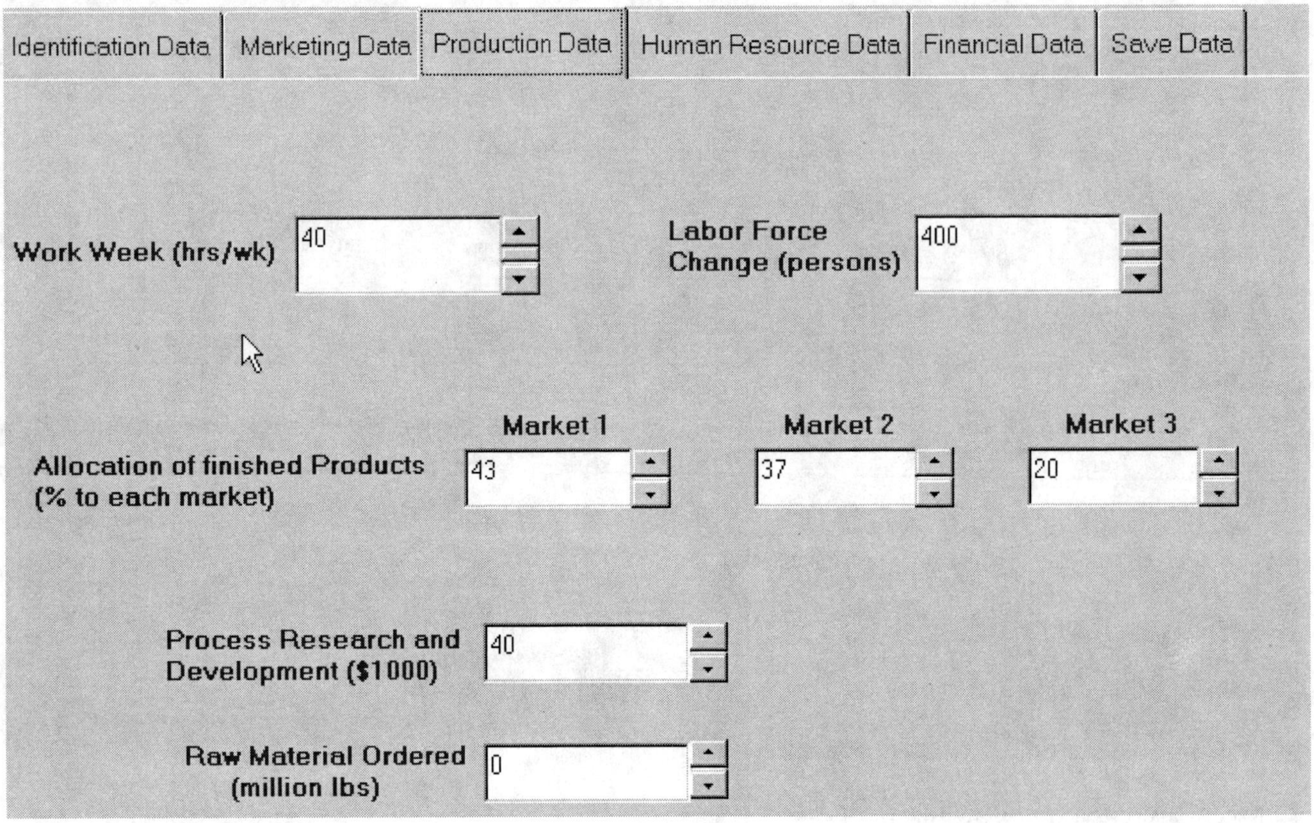

Identification Data	Marketing Data	Production Data	Human Resource Data	Financial Data	Save Data

Work Week (hrs/wk) `40`

Labor Force
Change (persons) `400`

	Market 1	Market 2	Market 3
Allocation of finished Products (% to each market)	`43`	`37`	`20`

Process Research and
Development ($1000) `40`

Raw Material Ordered
(million lbs) `0`

Enter your Production Decisions in the
appropriate windows and check them for
accuracy. When you finish, **click on Human
Resources.**

Figure 4-5
Human Resources Data Menu

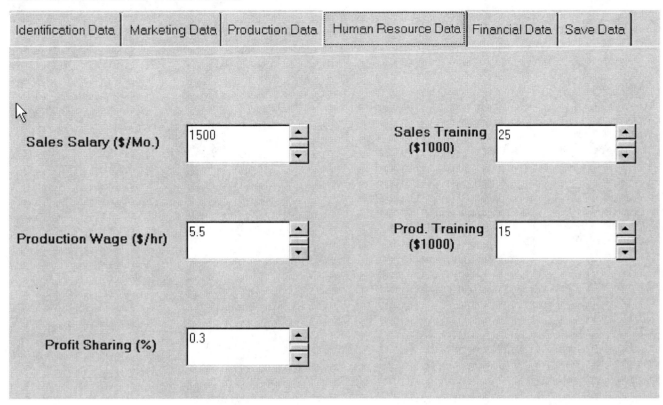

Enter your Human Resources Decisions in the
appropriate windows and check them for
accuracy. When you finish, **click on the
Financial Data.**

Figure 4-6
Financial/Accounting Data Menu

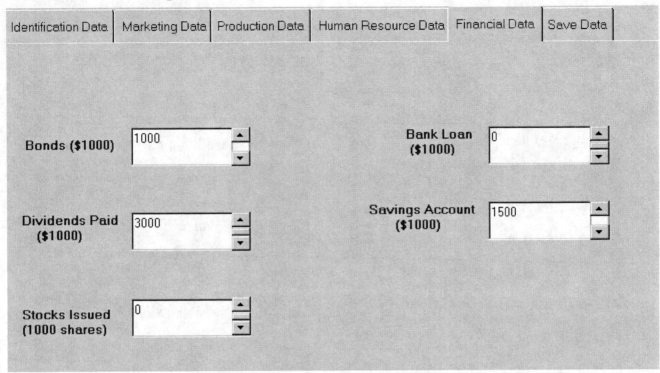

| Identification Data | Marketing Data | Production Data | Human Resource Data | Financial Data | Save Data |

Bonds ($1000) `1000`

Bank Loan ($1000) `0`

Dividends Paid ($1000) `3000`

Savings Account ($1000) `1500`

Stocks Issued (1000 shares) `0`

Enter your Financial/Accounting Decisions in the appropriate windows and check them for accuracy. When you finish, **click on Save Data.**

Figure 4-7
Save Data Menu

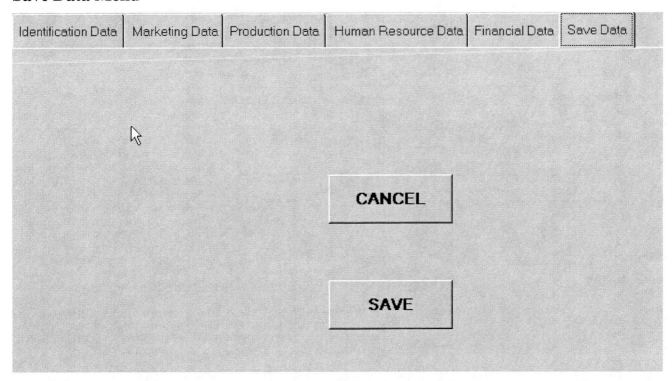

Now **click on "Save"**. If you have not violated any of the limits (identified in Table 3-2), you will be returned to the BUSPOG Main Menu.

The limits on entries (presented in Table 3-2) are placed in the program to detect errors in entries They do *not* mean you should *not* invest more than this amount in a variable. In some cases it may be necessary in order to achieve the best results for maintaining your competitive position.

If you receive an error message regarding one or more of your entries and you intend to exceed this limit with your investment, ask your game administrator to override the limitation.

Receiving an error message should provide a signal that until the error is corrected (or until your game administrator has provided an override), you have not saved your new decisions . To avoid having to reenter your new decisions, correct any errors by using the **View Previous Quarter Data** option on the BUSPOG **Main Menu**.

The BUSPOG screen **View And Edit Data** provides the opportunity to check your entries in each of the functional areas. Feel free to change any of these entries. Changes will be made when you click the red DONE button.

If you had an error message after trying to save your original inputs, these errors will be shown in red on the View and Edit DATA screen.

Figure 4-8
View and Edit DATA Menu

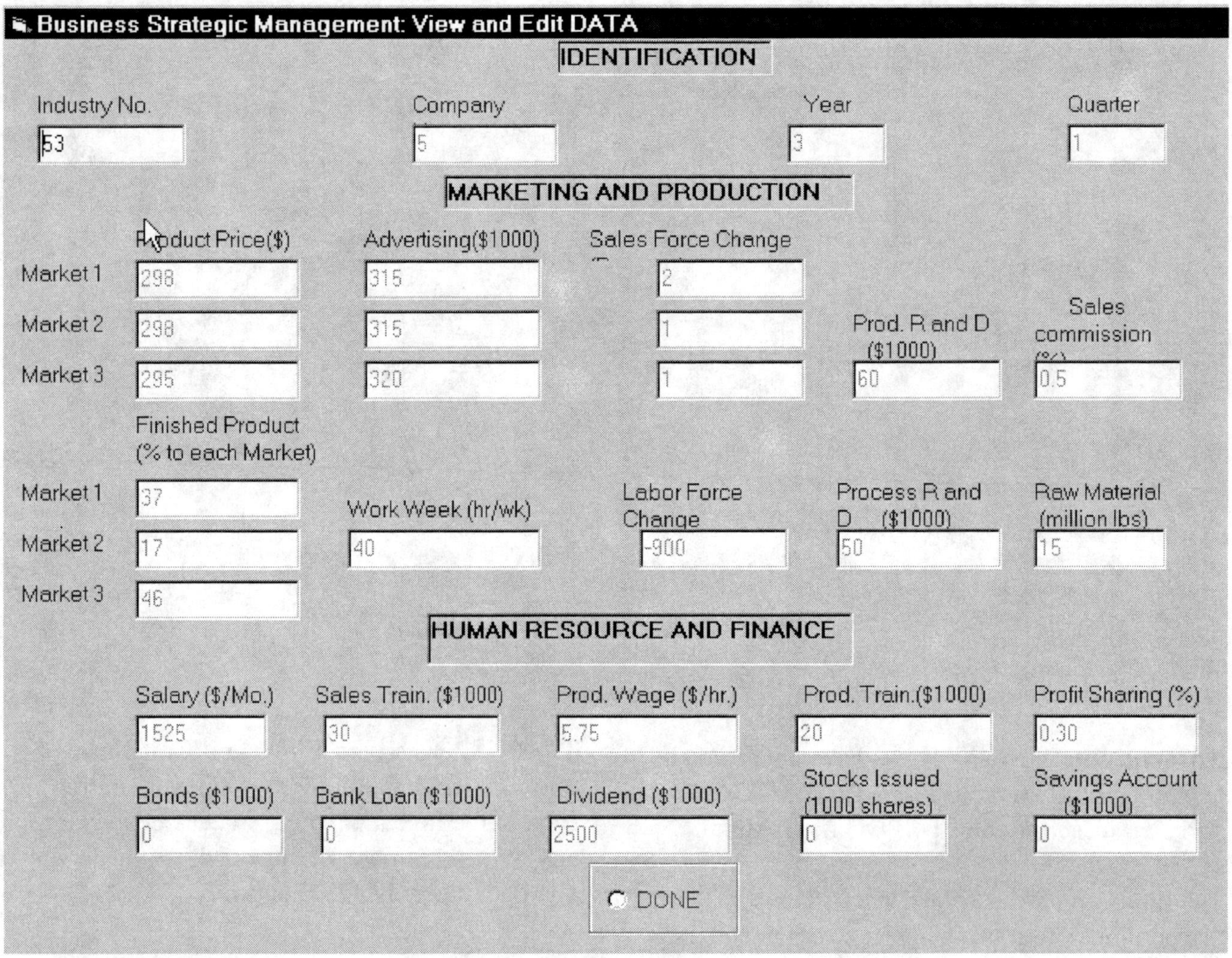

Once the entries are as you want them, click the red DONE button, and you will be returned to the BUSPOG **Main Menu**.

If for some purpose you would like to view data from a previous quarter, start from the BUSPOG **Main Menu**, choose **View Previous Quarter Data**, and the **BUSPOG Open File** will appear. Near the bottom of this screen there is a window labeled **Files of type,** and in the window you will see ***.inp**. At this point you can view input files only, but this will not always be the case.

Figure 4-9
BUSPOG Open File Menu

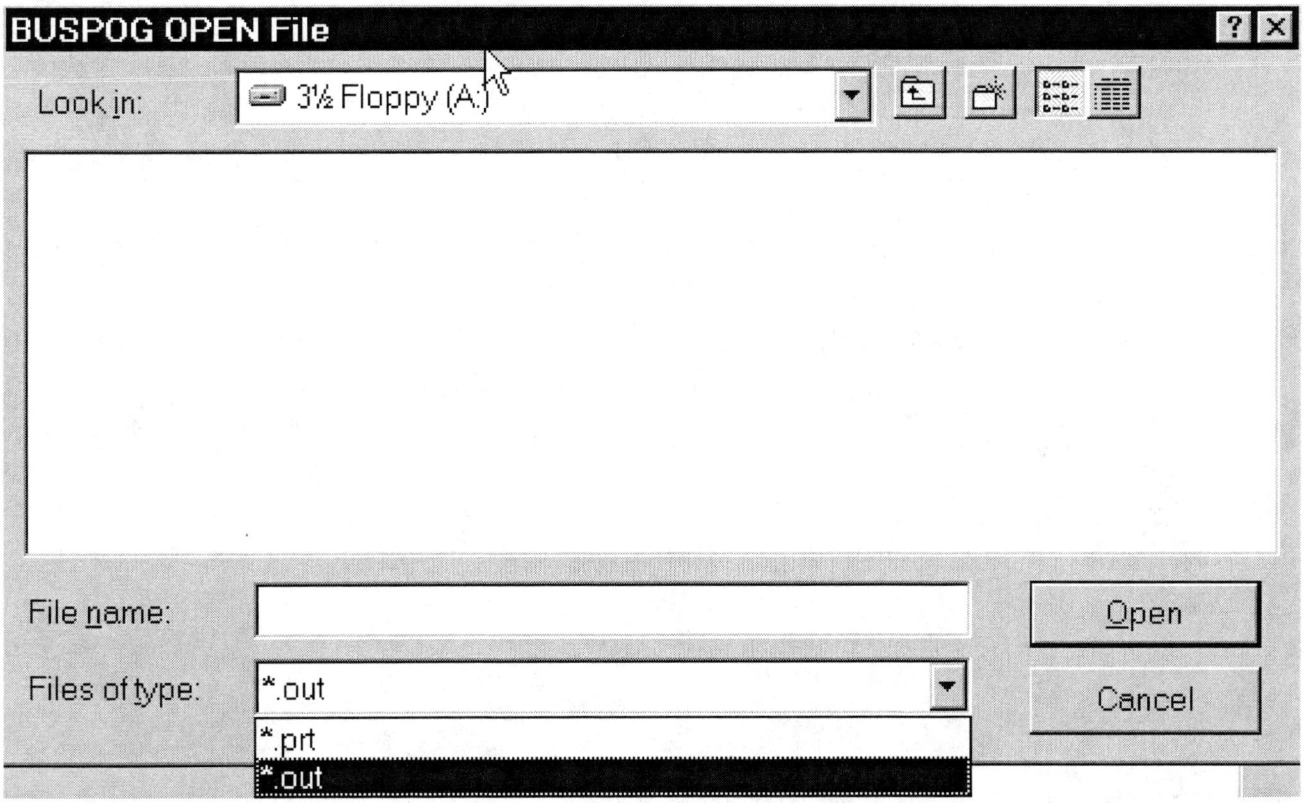

The large window near the top of this screen is labeled **Look in:** listed in the window are all of the input files you have saved so far. The format for this series of listings is F_(Industry)_(Team)_(Year)_(Quarter).

Number Number Number Number
Select the file that you want to view (that file name will appear in the window labeled **File name:**) then click on the **open** button, and your desired file will appear. When you are ready, click the red **DONE** button, and you will be returned to the BUSPOG **Main Menu**.

There are several reasons you might want to print either an input or an output file. You may want a paper record of your inputs in case you need to prove what you wanted your inputs to be. Some of your team members may want their own copies of a particular output report. In any case, start from the BUSPOG **Main Menu**. Select the **Print Input or Output File** option and again the **BUSPOG open File** will appear. This time all of

the input files have a **.prt** extension and the default value showing in the window is **.prt**. Click on the arrow by the **Files of type:** window, and you will find there are two types of files: inputs (**.prt**) and outputs (**.out**). If you want to print an input file, select **.prt**. If you want to print an outfile, select **.out**. When you select **.prt,** all of the input files are listed in the big window in the same format described previously. When you select **.out**, all of the output files are listed in the same format.

When you find the input or output file you want to print, click on the **Open** button. The Windows95® **Print** menu will appear. On this menu you can make any necessary adjustment to **Properties** or **Copies**, then click the **OK** button. The desired report(s) should be printed, and you will return to the BUSPOG **Main Menu**.

When you have finished, select **EXIT** and you will leave the BUSPOG program.

Interpreting Your First Results

5

After you have determined how you want to change what previous management was doing and have entered these decisions on your disk, the game administer collects disks from each team in your industry. (This procedure may be modified slightly if input computers are networked.)

Once they are available, the twenty decisions of each competing management team are processed through the computer-based BUSPOG simulation and the results of the competition for the quarter are reported to each company on computer-printed output reports. These results depend not only on a management team's decisions but also on the external environment, which includes the Task Environment (the BUSPOG company's customers, competitors, suppliers), and the Economic Environment.

Specifically, each team receives an OUTPUT REPORT which has six sections:

1. A DECISION REPORT lists the decisions made by the Top Management Team and includes any changes in the decisions made by the computer program because an input restriction was not followed.

2. A PRODUCTION AND SALES REPORT, which includes a summary of the Production Output and Sales Results for the company.

3. A COST REPORT, which includes Production, Marketing, and Other Costs for the company.

4. A FINANCIAL STATEMENT REPORT, which includes an Income Statement, Flow of Funds Statement, and Financial Position Statement for the company.

5. ECONOMY AND STOCK MARKET REPORT includes economic indicators for the industry, and stock market, earnings, dividends, and interest rates for all of the competing companies.

6. INDUSTRY ESTIMATE REPORT gives estimated values for a number of key variables for all of the companies in the industry.

An example of a computer-generated OUTPUT REPORT is presented as Figure 5-1. In reality this is more than an example since it is the actual report for Year 2, Quarter 4 which is the starting point for the first round of play.

Figure 5-1
Output Report: Year 2 Qtr. 4

COMPANY 1   INDUSTRY 1   YEAR 2   QUARTER 4

1. DECISIONS

	MARKET 1	MARKET 2	MARKET 3
PRICE ($/UNIT)	300.	300.	300.
ADVERTISING ($1000/QTR.)	300.	300.	300.
SALES FORCE CHANGE (NO.)	2	0	3
PRODUCT R & D ($1000/QTR.)	50.		
SALES COMMISSION (%)	0.4		
PROFIT SHARING (%)	0.3		
SALES SALARIES ($/MONTH)	1500.		
SALES TRAINING ($1000/QTR.)	25.		
PRODUCTION TRAINING ($1000/QTR.)	15.		
PRODUCTION WAGES ($/HR.)	5.50		
PRODUCTION SCHEDULED (HOURS/WEEK)	40.		
LABOR FORCE CHANGE (NO.)	400		
ALLOCATION TO MARKETS (%)	43.	37.	20.
PROCESS R & D ($1000/QTR.)	40.		
RAW MATERIALS ORDERED (MILLION LBS.)	0.		
BONDS SOLD OR REDEEMED ($1000)	0.		
BANK LOAN REQUESTED ($1000)	0.		
DIVIDENDS PAID ($1000)	3000.		
STOCK ISSUED(1000 SHARES)	0.		
SAVINGS ACCOUNT ($1000)	1500.		

2. PRODUCTION AND SALES

	MARKET 1	MARKET 2	MARKET 3	TOTAL
PRODUCTION WORKFORCE (NO.)	4000			
PRODUCTIVITY (UNITS/MAN-HOUR)	0.069			
RAW MATERIAL REQUIREMENTS (LBS./UNIT)	224.			
PRODUCTION OUTPUT (NO. OF UNITS)	62081	53419	28875	144375
FIN PROD INVENTORY (NO. UNITS)	56008	63318	1907	121233
RAW MAT INVENTORY (MILLION LBS.)	61.581			
DEMAND (NO. OF UNITS ORDERED)	72822	61900	37907	172629
SALES (NO. OF UNITS SOLD)	72822	61900	37907	172629
SALES ($1000)	21847.	18570.	11372.	51789.
SALESMEN ACTIVE (NO.)	22	24	9	55
SALES TRAINEES (NO.)	2	0	3	5

3. COSTS

PRODUCTION ($1000)		MARKETING ($1000)		OTHER ($1000)	
LABOR	11440.	ADVERTISING	900.	R & D	90.
MATERIAL	13509.	SALARIES	270.	CARRYING-FIN PROD	598.
MAINTENANCE	1716.	COMMISSIONS	207.	CARRYING-RAW MAT	376.
TRAINING	15.	TRANSPORTATION	1229.	BOND INTEREST	750.
PROD LEVEL CHANGE	401.	ADMINISTRATIVE	2963.	LOAN INTEREST	488.
EQUIPMENT	1351.	SALES FORCE CHANGE	42.	ADMINISTRATIVE	4807.
ADMINISTRATIVE	1122.	TRAINING	25.	BOND CALL PREMIUM	0.
DEPRECIATION	475.				
TOTAL	30028.	TOTAL	5636.	TOTAL	7109.

COMPANY 1 INDUSTRY 1 YEAR 2 QUARTER 4

4. FINANCIAL STATEMENTS

INCOME STATEMENT ($1000)

GROSS SALES REVENUE	51789.
BEGINNING INVENTORY	27968.
TOTAL PRODUCTION COST	30028.
GOODS AVAILABLE	57996.
ENDING INVENTORY	25008.
COST OF GOODS SOLD	32988.
GROSS PROFIT	18800.
TOTAL MARKETING COST	5636.
PROFIT ON SALES	13165.
TOTAL OTHER COST	7109.
TOTAL OTHER INCOME	20.
NET PROFIT BFOR TAXES	6076.
INCOME TAXES	3038.
PROFIT SHARING COST	9.
NET INCOME	3029.
DIVIDENDS PAID	3000.
RETAINED EARNINGS	29.

FLOW OF FUNDS STATEMENT ($1000)

ACCOUNTS COLLECTED	53746.
BANK LOANS REQUESTED	0.
BOND SALE RETURN	0.
SAV ACCT-INT & WITHDRAWAL	20.
PLANT & EQUIP. SALE	0.
STOCK SALE RETURN	0.
BEGINNING CASH	433.
TOTAL SOURCES	54199.
TOTAL PRODUCTION COST	16045.
TOTAL MARKETING COST	5636.
TOTAL OTHER COST	7109.
DIVIDENDS PAID	3000.
LOAN REPAYMENT	15000.
BONDS REDEEMED	0.
INCOME TAXES	3038.
PROFIT SHARING COST	9.
PLANT & EQUIP. INVEST.	601.
SAVINGS ACCT. DEPOSIT	1500.
TOTAL DISBURSEMENTS	51937.
CASH AVAILABLE	2262.
EMERGENCY BANK LOAN	0.
CASH BALANCE	2262.

FINANCIAL POSITION STATEMENT ($1000)

CASH BALANCE	2262.
ACCOUNTS RECEIVABLE	17263.
INVENTORY-FIN. PROD.	25008.
INVENTORY-RAW MAT.	25722.
SAVINGS ACCT BALANCE	2500.
TOTAL CURRENT ASSETS	72754.
PLANT & EQUIP. VALUE	47625.
TOTAL ASSETS	120379.
BANK LOAN BALANCE	0.
BONDS OUTSTANDING	30000.
CAPITAL STOCK VALUE	63045.
ACCUM. RET. EARNINGS	27334.
TOTAL STOCK. EQUITY	90379.
TOTAL LIABILITIES	120379.

5. ECONOMY AND STOCK MARKET

GROSS NATIONAL PRODUCT 173. ($BILLIONS)
NUMBER OF HOUSEHOLD FORMATIONS 383. (1000.S)
PERSONAL CONSUMPTION EXP.—DURABLES 13. ($BILLIONS)
RAW MATERIAL COST 0.49 ($/LB.)

COMPANY	STOCK PRICE	EARNINGS	DIVIDENDS	SHARES	PROD. WAGES	SALES SALARIES	BOND INTEREST	LOAN INTEREST
LOSSES UNLIMITED, INC.	10.51	0.50	0.50	6000.	5.65	1485.	10.0	13.0
UNAWESOME FOURSOME ASSN.	10.51	0.50	0.50	6000.	5.45	1453.	10.0	13.0
BOZO PRODUCTIONS	10.51	0.50	0.50	6000.	5.59	1419.	10.0	13.0
DIVERSIFIED, INC.	10.51	0.50	0.50	6000.	5.64	1423.	10.0	13.0
THE SYNDICATE	10.51	0.50	0.50	6000.	5.55	1564.	10.0	13.0
THE BENDOKEMPF CORP.	10.51	0.50	0.50	6000.	5.70	1458.	10.0	13.0
UNETHICAL, INC.	10.51	0.50	0.50	6000.	5.66	1491.	10.0	13.0

6. INDUSTRY ESTIMATES

COMPANY	AVERAGE PRICE	AVERAGE ADVERT.	SALES COMM.	PROFIT SHARING	PROD. WORKFORCE	PROD. OUTPUT	SALES FORCE	UNIT SALES
LOSSES UNLIMITED, INC.	312.	288.	0.39	0.30	3790	139474	52	170111
UNAWESOME FOURSOME ASSN.	312.	304.	0.41	0.29	4158	144157	55	169906
BOZO PRODUCTIONS	306.	299.	0.40	0.30	3831	141421	53	172302
DIVERSIFIED, INC.	319.	296.	0.40	0.30	3957	141646	53	163998
THE SYNDICATE	287.	315.	0.40	0.30	3856	141895	56	169502
THE BENDOKEMPF CORP.	299.	312.	0.42	0.28	3999	147032	54	179980
UNETHICAL, INC.	290.	301.	0.39	0.30	4078	143191	57	173682

The Top Management Team of each of the competing BUSPOG companies controls the operation of its company by selecting values for the twenty decision variables each quarter. Within the BUSPOG computer program the values selected by each team are combined with the effects of the Task Environment and the Economic Environment. The results of these computations are presented to each Top Management Team through the six sections of the OUTPUT REPORT. The data from this report are examined by the Top Management Team to determine if the value of one or more of the decision variables should be changed for the next quarter. The OUTPUT REPORT provides the feedback necessary for exercising managerial control over the company's operation.

The data of the first four sections of the OUTPUT REPORT summarize the results for the company itself--the Internal Environment. The data of the last two sections of the OUTPUT REPORT summarize the results for all the companies within the industry and the BUSPOG Task and Economic Environments. Appendix A presents the OUTPUT REPORT with these six sections for each company for the eight quarters prior to the initiation of competition, that is, for Year 1, Quarter 1 through Year 2, Quarter 4. You may wish to refer to that appendix while reading the remainder of this chapter.

Internal Environment

The first section of the OUTPUT REPORT is the DECISION REPORT. It presents the decisions that were used by the computer program for a company. This report allows the company's Top Management to check that its intended decisions were used and to determine if any of its decisions were altered by the computer program because they violated the restrictions on the input values (see Decision Variable Summary, Table 3-1).

Next is the PRODUCTION AND SALES REPORT, which summarizes many important aspects of these two business functions:

1. The number of employees in the Production Workforce at the end of the last quarter
2. The Productivity in units per person-hour during the last quarter
3. The Raw Materials Requirements in pounds per unit of Finished Product during the last quarter
4. The Production output for all Three Markets during the last quarter
5. The number of units in the Finished Product Inventory for all Three Markets at the end of the last quarter
6. The Raw Materials Inventory in millions of pounds at the end of the last quarter, including the Raw Materials ordered last quarter
7. The number of units of Finished Product Demanded for all Three Markets during the last quarter
8. The number of units of Sold for all Three Markets during the last quarter
9. The Sales in dollars for all Three Markets during the last quarter
10. The number of Active Salespersons for all Three Markets at the end of the last quarter
11. The number of Sales Trainees who will become Active Sales Persons at the beginning of the next quarter for all Three Markets

The third section of the OUTPUT REPORT, the COSTS REPORT presents a compilation of the Production, Marketing, and Other Costs. These costs are computed from an income basis as opposed to a cash flow basis. This means that the Production cost includes an entry for depreciation, and the Raw Materials cost is an evaluation of the raw material used for Production during the quarter, not ordered during the quarter. Further details regarding the computation of these costs are provided in Chapter 10.

The fourth section of the OUTPUT REPORT is the FINANCIAL STATEMENT REPORT. This report includes an Income Statement, a Flow Of Funds Statement, and a Financial Position Statement. These statements are commensurate with usual accounting practice (discussed in conjunction with Tables 10-1 through 10-4, Chapter 10).

Task and Economic Environments

At the top of the fifth section of the OUTPUT REPORT, the ECONOMY AND STOCK MARKET REPORT, are the values at the end of the last quarter for the three BUSPOG economic variables: Gross Domestic Product, and Personal Consumption Expenditures for Durables (in billions of dollars), and the Number Of Household Formations (in thousands of units). This fifth section also gives the Cost of Raw Material (in dollars per pound) for the upcoming quarter. A listing of values follows for each of the competing companies for six variables. These include:

1. The Price of a Share of Common Stock at the end of the last quarter (in dollars)
2. The Earnings per Share of Common Stock during the last quarter (in dollars)
3. The Dividends per Share of Common Stock during the last quarter (in dollars)
4. The Number of Shares of Common Stock Outstanding at the end of the last quarter
5. The Bond Interest Rate at the end of the last quarter (in percentage)
6. The short-term (three-month) Loan Interest Rate at the end of the last quarter (in percentage)

The final section, the INDUSTRY ESTIMATES REPORT, presents estimated values for ten key variables for all the companies in the BUSPOG industry. These are the type of data that might be available from market research or other industry sources and should be considered only as rough estimates of the actual values. An indication of the amount of error in these estimates can be obtained by a company by comparing the known values for its own variables with the estimated values given in this report. The variables for which estimates are given include:

1. The Unit Selling Price during the last quarter (in dollars), averaged over the Three Markets
2. The Advertising Expenditures during the last quarter, averaged over all three markets (in thousands of dollars)

3. The Sales Commission Percentage paid by each company during the last quarter
4. The profit-sharing percentage during the last quarter
5. The monthly Salary for a salesperson during the last quarter (in dollars)

6. The hourly Production Wage Rate during the last quarter (in dollars)
7. The number of persons in the Production Workforce at the end of the last quarter
8. The total Production Output during the last quarter (in units)
9. The total number of active Salespersons at the end of the last quarter
10. The total number of units of Finished Product sold during the last quarter

Interpreting the OUTPUT REPORT

When you first look at an OUTPUT REPORT, you may find it a confusing array of numbers, but you will soon come to realize that seasoned managers use such reports to evaluate not only where they are but also how they can get where they want to be.

Look now at your OUTPUT REPORT. Identify the six sections of the report and review the descriptions of each.

Look next at the first section, DECISIONS, which presents what the computer accepted at your team's first set of decisions. Check this data to be sure you did not make any mistakes as you entered your decisions. Also check to see if BUSPOG made any changes. If there are any questions, bring them up immediately because you can rely on BUSPOG continuing with the same calculation time after time. If you had results you did not anticipate, most likely it was due to your misunderstanding some aspect of the game.

You probably would like to see now if you made any profit in this quarter. This will be found in Section 4, FINANCIAL STATEMENTS. Profit is called *Net Income* in BUSPOG, and is reported near the bottom of the Income Statement. Check not only the actual numbers reported but also the units of these numbers. For example, since all financial information is reported in thousands, you will need to add three zeros to the numbers. (In the Report for year 2, Quarter 4 , Figure 5-1, *Net Income* is reported to have been 3029; it is actually $3,029,000)

Next, check the condition of your cash account. The prime responsibility of your CFO (Chief Financial Officer) is to insure that you earned enough cash to cover all of the expenditures you authorized. Your Cash Balance is presented at the bottom of the Flow Of Funds Statement, the second statement in *Section 4*. Notice on the line two levels above your Cash Balance is Cash Available. If your Cash Available is positive, you had enough cash to pay all of your bills; that number is also your Cash Balance.

Like any good CFO, the previous Vice-President of Finance negotiated a line of credit with your bank to be drawn upon whenever the company might need extra cash. It is called an Emergency Bank Loan. If Cash Available is negative, an Emergency Bank Loan had to be initiated to cover the overdraft' it will be added to other Bank Loans Requested.

Contrary to the opinion of most students at the beginning of this game, bankers do not penalize a company by raising its interest rate when there is an increase in Loans Outstanding. Bankers want companies to make loans because that is how they make money themselves. What bankers avoid is making loans to companies which don't repay them. They generally assume that CFOs who can't manage their cash are not very good financial managers and loans made to these companies are more risky than loans made to companies with competent financial managers. As noted in the discussion of Task Environment, your banker in BUSPOG will always honor your request for an Emergency Bank Loan, but the banker will increase the interest you must pay because you demonstrated an inadequate ability to manage your finances.

When an Emergency Bank Loan is required, your loan interest increases significantly. This is not true when you request a Bank Loan; it demonstrates you are adequately planning and managing your finances.

Look now at Section 5, ECONOMY AND STOCK MARKET REPORT. Compare your Stock Price to the prices of your competitors. Some investors in stock value a particular stock because it will provide income for living expenses; the company can be relied on to pay divi-dends. Others value particular stock because the company is holding profits earned as Accumulated Retained Earnings (These are referred to as capital gains especially by taxing authorities.)

In BUSPOG, the value of your company in the eyes of your stockholders can be assessed by multiplying Stock Price times the number of Shares Outstanding. (Note: in Section 5, Shares are reported in thousands; add three zeroes.)

To interpret and compare your company's results, consider the difference between Year 2, Quarter 4 results presented in Figure 5-1 and the results in the report for Year 3, Quarter 1. Remember every company began the game in the same position. All the entries in Section 5 of the OUTPUT REPORT for Year 2, Quarter 4 should be the same--and they are. For Year 3, Quarter 1 and throughout the remainder of the game they will be different..

Go back to Section 2, PRODUCTION AND SALES REPORT. This section provides detailed information about the effectiveness of your Marketing and Production program.

The data are provided in four columns. Results are reported for individual markets as Market 1,

Market 2, and Market 3. Sometimes the same information is summarized in a Total column.

If results are reported in only the first column, the information applies to the whole company. For example, the first entry in Section 2 tells you how many people you have in your Production Workforce. Since all production personnel work in your factory and you have only one factory, there is only one Production Workforce. Check this number to be sure the number of Production Workers is what you expected (the number you had last quarter modified by the labor force change you requested in your decisions). If it is not, it is probably lower than you anticipated and this indicates that some of your production workers voluntarily quit.

Productivity tells you the number of Finished Products you will get for each production hour during the quarter. While the absolute level is important (the higher the productivity, the lower the cost of each Finished Product), it is also important at this stage of the game to note changes in your level of productivity. Is it going up or is it going down? How fast is it changing? If it is going down, it means you are not investing enough in building your productivity. If it is going up, you may be satisfied with the rate of change (which means you will maintain your present level of investments in productivity). If you want it to go up faster, you may want to increase them.

Raw Material Requirements indicate the number of pounds of raw material it takes to make one Finished Product. Raw Material Requirements are inversely related to Productivity. Investments which build Productivity also reduce Raw Materials Requirements.

Production Output is the number of units you made last quarter (in the TOTAL column). This line also tells you how many Finished Units were transported to the warehouse in each market. Information presented on this line will become more useful as you gain experience with BUSPOG.

The next line, Finished Product Inventory, indicates the number of videocassette recorders you have left in each warehouse at the end of the quarter. This is very important information because you want enough inventory left in each market to cover any inaccuracy in your calculations. On the other hand, you don't want too much because you must pay to store units which remain in your warehouse at the end of the quarter.

You can get an idea of how appropriate your inventory is if you divide the number of units left in your ending Finished Product inventory by the number of units sold by your salespeople in that market (Demand). The result will be the proportion of Demand that remains in your inventory. In other words, if Demand is the same next quarter you already have this much left over to ship out. If you subtract this figure from 100, you will learn how much of next quarter's Demand will be met by new production. As you may know, the practice of Just-in-time Inventory Control calls for selling product as close as possible to date of production to minimize Ending Inventories.

It is also wise to compare the percentage of Demand which remains in each market in order to check your decisions on Allocations.

The next two lines, Demand and Sales (units) should be considered at the same time. Remember that Demand is the number of customers who said "send me one". Sales, on the other hand are the orders you filled--the number you delivered to customers. If the two numbers are the same, you delivered all the units that were ordered and you probably have units left in your Finished Product Inventory. If Sales are less than Demand, it means you did not have enough Finished Product to fill all your orders--you stocked out. In BUSPOG when you stock out part, half of the shortfall remains as back orders which will be filled from the first new production. (As such they must be added to the forecast of Demand for next quarter.) The other half of the stockout will be distributed to the other companies in your industry, and you lose these customers permanently.

The next line, Sales ($1,000) reports the amount of cash generated by your sales activity in this market (unit sales are multiplied by the price in that market).

The next line Salesmen Active indicates the number of active salespeople you have in each market as well as the total. This number should equal the number of Salespeople you had last quarter plus the number of Sales Trainees. If is does not, the difference is probably negative and indicates the number of Salespeople who voluntarily quit.

Sales Trainees should reflect your decisions on Sales Force Change.

Move now to Section 6, INDUSTRY ESTI-MATES. All the other sections of the OUTPUT REPORT present very precise accounting-quality data in the data. Section 6, however, are much less precise, they are only approximate. You can find out for yourself how far off they are by comparing the information about your company presented in the first five sections to the information presented in Section 6. For example, calculate your real average price indicated by your decisions in Section 1. Subtract the Average Price reported for your company in Section 6, Divide that difference by your real average price. The difference will probably not be far beyond 5%.

Now compare the information about your company with the information about your competitors. Compare their strategy with yours. What are they doing about pricing, advertising, motivation, and wages? Compare the size of their Production Workforce and their Sales Force to the sizes of your own. You can get a rough idea about their Productivity by dividing each company's Production Output by the size of their Production Work force which will give you output per worker). Similarly, you can get a rough idea of the effectiveness of their sales program by dividing their unit sales by the number of people

in their Sales Force which will give you the number of sales each salesperson is making.

Finally, from the data in Section 6 you can estimate Market Share. First, add together the total Unit Sales to get the size of your industry's market. Now, divide the Unit Sales reported for each company by Total Sales and multiply by 100. You will get each company's percentage of the market --the usually accepted definition of Market Share. It is not only the number that is important but also the way it is moving. The latter indicates the relative effectiveness of your sales program.

Managing Your Growth

6

In the real world, management can be either the greatest strength or the greatest weakness an organization possesses because the organization's activities for the most part are determined by the decisions and actions of management. In the BUSPOG world, this statement is even more true. At the beginning of competition, the only difference between the competing companies is their management. The productivity of the labor force, the effectiveness of the sales force, the financial resources available to the firm, and all other factors are the same. As the game progresses, differences in these factors develop. These differences result exclusively from the decisions of each company's Top Management Team. Therefore, to achieve the best outcomes for your company, carefully and thoroughly evaluate and plan your managerial decision making.

If you don't know where you're going, any road will do. Suppose you are the captain of a cruise ship, and you are told to take that ship from Los Angeles to Tokyo Bay. If you take off without planning how to accomplish this assignment, the chances of your getting there are very poor indeed. In fact not only should you know where you are going (your *goal*) and when you are supposed to get there, but also the means to be used and when. You should probably treat each of these means as a subgoal and plan how you will achieve each. If you are like most captains, ultimately you will have goals, means, and schedules for each week of your trip, for each day of the first week, and even for each hour of the first day.

In addition, each of the ship's functional divisions (engineering, dining, navigation, communication, housekeeping, etc.) will have its own goals,

means, and schedules through which the overall goals, means, and schedules will be achieved.

This example is suggested to demonstrate the importance of planning not only where you want to go but when you want to get there, selecting not only how you will accomplish this but when you will complete each of the steps. You can redefine means as the goals for shorter time-frames or smaller organizational units. You can plan until you have goals and schedules for every unit in your organization and every time-frame in your planning process.

This example demonstrates the importance of planning:
1. Identify your goals
2. Identify when each goal must/should/could be achieved.
3. Select means for achieving each goal.
4. Identify when each mean must/should/could be completed.

In short, if you want your company to become all it can be, you must manage your future.

The Top Management Team of an organization is responsible for its total operations including its growth. The total operations for a BUSPOG company are shown in Figure 6-1. This conceptualization does not show all the relationships and elements among the company's operations, only the major ones. As indicated in the figure, the Top Management Team is not only concerned with the company's internal operations but also its interfaces with the external environment.

Figure 6-1
Functional Organizational Structure

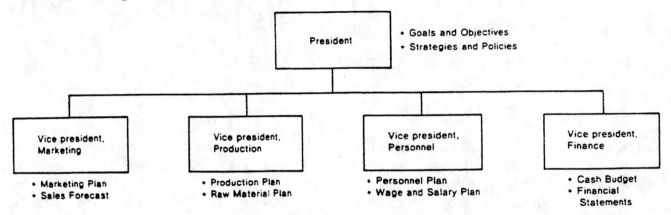

In this chapter we will focus on the planning and preparation for decision-making that must be done by the Top Management Team of a BUSPOG company.

Organizational structure

A team's first step in managing the company's growth is to **decide on an organizational structure** for the company. At the beginning of play, management team members should clearly delineate responsibilities and procedures to be followed in preparing and submitting decisions and any reports required by the game administrator. Since the specification of responsibilities in the organizational structure affects how well the team members work together, this first step in planning is an important one. Later in the play, when everyone is familiar with the details of the game, the team may want to modify this organizational structure to provide more consensus in decision-making. Unless the game administrator specifies the organizational structure to be used, the team can adopt whatever structure seems most appropriate. There is considerable wisdom in cross-training team members in all functional positions as soon as possible in order to compensate for unanticipated absences.

A functional organization similar to that depicted in Figure 6-1 is the most usual organizational structure selected by BUSPOG teams. This structure lends itself to a clear specification of the responsibilities for making and submitting the twenty decisions required from the team each quarter. In such a functional organizational structure, each vice-president is responsible for a set of five decisions in his or her functional area; the president (if you have one) assumes responsibility for coordinating the decisions of the vice presidents to insure the decisions support the company's goals and objectives. Again, there are distinct advantages in cross-training, in cross-checking to avoid errors, and in combining the intuition and knowledge of all members of the team.

If a management team is made up of more or less than five members and a functional structure is desired, the responsibilities in the functional areas can be either combined or shared to fit the situation. For example, if a company has four members, the responsibilities of one of the vice presidents can be assumed by all four members or by only three of them. If a team has more than five members, the responsibilities of one or more of the vice presidents can be shared.

In addition to specifying the decision-making responsibilities, the organizational structure delineates the responsibilities for preparing and submitting reports to the game administrator.

Figure 6-1 indicates some of the reporting responsibilities for each position.

Planning Data Base

The second step in planning is to **decide which data are important to the planning process**. While the planning process depends heavily on the availability and utilization of information, not all the information available is equally important. In the real world, the potential factors to be included in the planning data base are essentially unlimited and a process called *Environmental Scanning* is used to focus on only that information that is important to the organization. Although the factors that can be included in the simulated world of BUSPOG are limited, even here not all of the information is equally important.

The planning information a company needs can be classified into four broad types:
1. Industry environment
2. Internal situation
3. Task environment
4. Broad or macro environment
(You may recall this is the structure used in Chapter 2.)

Industry Environment:

While all of the companies in the industry start from the same position at the beginning of play, the planning data base will change as the competition progresses. The set of critical factors identified by the Top Management Team before the competition begins will be altered as additional information becomes available and as relative strengths and weaknesses develop. There are reasons some teams do better than others. Discovering these reasons is one of the major tasks of management.

In addition to these differences among the management teams in your industry, some aspects of the industry will change and need to be recog-

nized. One of these is the size of the total market for videocassette recorders. The effectiveness of your marketing program may seem quite acceptable if you only watch your level of sales, but you must also watch your market share. If your total market grows a lot and your sales don't grow as fast, a drop in market share may be the only sign you'll get that your Marketing program is not competitive. Similarly, you may find it much easier to forecast demand in your Three Markets if you can figure out where your product is on a product life cycle curve.

Internal Situation

The Internal-Planning Data-Base can include any of the company data that are given in the first four sections of the Output Report. For example, it should include the twenty decision variables and the additional variables reported for the company in the Production and Sales Report, the Cost Report, and the Financial Statements. In addition, there are two variables from the fifth section of the (Economy and Stock Market Output Report which should be considered:
1. Bond Interest charged the next quarter
2. Loan Interest charged the next quarter

Each company's management will have to evaluate each variable carefully and select those data that will be useful for planning, implementing and controlling goal-achievement. With experience and the understanding that results, your team can use increasing amounts of information generated through increasingly sophisticated procedures.

Task Environment

The Task Environment of an individual company includes competitors, customers, suppliers and the technology which the BUSPOG company is using. While Top management undoubtedly wants accurate values for all of the items in all of the sections of the Output Report, it is quite unlikely that accounting-quality information on all competitor operations will be available

Nevertheless, management can obtain additional accurate values for items reported in the fifth section, the Economy and Stock Market Report and fairly accurate data from the sixth section, Industry Estimates.

The Economy and Stock Market Report gives accurate information about six variables for all the BUSPOG companies:
1. Stock price
2. Earnings per share
3. Dividends per share
4. Shares of Stock outstanding
5. Bond Interest
6. Loan Interest

In addition, the Planning Data Base can include any of the Task Environment's variables reported in Section 6, Industry Estimates:
1. Average Price
2. Average Advertising
3. Sales Commission
4. Profit-Sharing
5. Sales Salaries
6. Production Wages
7. Production Work Force
8. Production Output
9. Sales Force
10. Unit Sales

It must be remembered that the data of the Industry Estimates, the sixth section of the Output Report, are not as accurate as the data in the first five sections. They are not *accounting-quality information.*

Again, management may not wish to consider all these factors just because they are available. The benefit of including each depends on your team's ability to manage the company. The value of the data will have to be compared with the cost in effort to obtain and use them.

Broad or Macro Environment

The Broad Environment includes all aspects of an organization's External Environment that are not included in the Task Environment. In the real world the Broad Environment includes laws and government programs, the social and cultural factors which influence a company, and economic growth which affects customers and suppliers.

The Broad Environment for the Planning Data Base of BUSPOG companies can include the four economic variables listed in the Economy and Stock Market Report:
1. Anticipated Gross Domestic Product
2. Anticipated Personal Consumption
3. Anticipated Household Formations
4. Raw Material Cost
Not all of these, however, are necessarily significant.

Goals and Objectives

If you don't know where you're going, any road will do. The only way to know which road to take is to know where each road will take you -- and to know where you want to go. Managers set goals and then use them as guides. In management theory, this is referred to as the *centrality of goals.*

The third step in planning for decision-making is to define and formulate your organization's *mission* and *vision,* and to identify and adopt *strategic, tactical, and operational goals.*

A company's *mission* is a basic statement of the reasons for the firm's existence -- some would say this is what you want to add to your society. Your *vision* is what you would like to become once you have enough time to be anything that is feasible. The term *strategic goals* refers to a series of events through which you believe you can achieve your mission and your vision. *Tactical goals* refers to the long-range results an organization desires. *Operational goals* are the short-range results that can be used to assess progress toward other organizational goals. In general, *operational goals* are more specific and are achieved in a shorter time period than the other goals.

Identifying and adopting goals and the means for achieving them is a very difficult process. Because every aspect interacts with every other aspect, the process can seem to be buzzing, booming confusion.

To begin to set goals and objectives, identify a set of *time-frames* for your planning in which one time-frame goes from the time the plan is adopted (the present) out one year. For now, call this period the *short-range*.

Now, choose another period of time that is an even multiple of the *short-range* (usually 3, 4, or 5 years). Call this period the *long-range*. Finally, choose another period of time that is an even multiple of the *long-range* (usually 3, 4, or 5 *long-range* periods). Call this period the *very-long-range*. The only constraint here is that the *very-long-range* must be long enough to get more of every resource that will be consumed by the **very-long-range** plans.

Figure 6-2
Goals and Means

Mission and Vision:

	Goals	Means
Very-Long-Range	**Strategic Goals**	**Strategies**
Long-Range	**Tactical Goals**	**Tactics**
Short-Range	**Operational Goals**	**Operations**

Before beginning the short-range time frame managers identify what must/should/could be different *at* the *end* of that one-year (*short-range*) time frame. The result is a set of *operational goals*.

In BUSPOG each company's performance is evaluated in comparison with the performance of every other company participating in the competition. This evaluation is based on a number of

criteria, including how well the management of the company has succeeded in attaining its goals. One of the initial tasks then for each Top Management Team is to formulate the *short-range* goals for the company and the means through which each goal will be accomplished.

All goals for a BUSPOG company as well as the means through which the goals will be achieved are specified by Top Management. Only after considering a number of elements that influence which goals can be attained, (in particular, competitors, customers, employees, raw-material suppliers, stockholders, and creditors,) do they adopt these goals and means.

Managers of real world organizations as well as simulated organizations, such as the BUSPOG companies, often state their organization's goals in very general terms. For example, "We wish to attain a maximum return for a minimum investment." Such a goal statement is not very useful in guiding management in formulating the appropriate strategies, tactics, operations, and policies to attain goals and objectives. To avoid such generalizations, formulate goals in terms that can be counted and measured and prepare a written statement of these goals. Only then can the level of attainment of any particular goal or objective be evaluated. This written statement is frequently referred to as the *strategic plan*.

Before moving on, one additional point should be made. There is a tendency to define a goal by the activities through which another goal will be achieved. Goals and objectives should always focus on the *outputs* which result from particular actions rather than the actions themselves. This is the only way to insure that your actions achieve your goals.

Top Management should choose the organization's goals and decide how and when to achieve them. Some of the factors in the game that can be used as goals include:

1. Productivity factors, such as units of finished product per Production Hour or Sales per Salesperson.
2. Financial ratios such as profitability ratios, sales to current asset ratios, Net Income to Total Stockholder's Equity ratios, or Return on Investment.
3. Growth factors, such as increases in Net Income, Sales Level, or Market Share.

In addition, you might state the goals regarding employees' welfare in terms of Sales Salaries or Production Wage Rates in relation to the levels prevailing in the industry.

Examples of possible goals for a BUSPOG company are given in Figure 6-3. Figure 6-4 also lists goals, but they are stated in a more sophisticated way. These goals were delineated in players' reports and are offered here as examples, rather than models to follow.

Figure 6-3
Examples of Goals

1. To gain and maintain at least 20% share of each product's market.
2. To provide a regular dividend and corporate growth yielding a cumulative return on initial investment of at least 8%.
3. To maintain a product price that does not exceed the market maximum.
4. To maintain a stable work environment for our employees (never firing anyone) through long-range production planning.
5. To continue to develop more salable products and more economical production methods (increasing sales/salesperson and productivity by 10% each quarter).

The operational goals of a company are short-term statements of outcomes that are to be achieved in one evaluation period. In BUSPOG, this period is one year. The list of criteria to use in formulating a statement of **operational goals** is presented in Table 6-5. Remember, this list is not meant to be exhaustive. The data necessary to compute values for all of these performance objectives are given in the BUSPOG output reports.

Figure 6-4
Tactical and Operational Goals

1. Market percentage: To recover the market share lost in Year 4. This would entail bringing our present market share from 15.82% to 16.14% by the end of year 5. Specific areas of concentration will be in Market 1 (where our goal will be 36%) and Market 3 (where our goal will be 17%). Market 2 is expected to remain at its present level.
2. Return on Investment: To pay a total of $2,400,000 to the stockholders, yielding a $0.40 per share dividend. In addition, the goal for Earnings per Share is $1.50.
3. Price: To maintain Product Price within 5% of the median price in each market.
4. Inventories: To schedule production in such a manner as to provide enough units for sale to meet Demand requirements plus maintain an Ending Inventory of no less than 150,000 units nor more than 300,000 units each quarter.
5. Research and Development: To continue an aggressive R&D program that will yield more saleable products as well as cost savings through production efficiencies so that Market Share will increase to 23% and Productivity will be .092 by the end of the year.

Strategies and Policies

Top Management's fourth step in planning for effective decision-making is to formulate the actual strategies, tactics, and operations to be used. The term *strategic goals* refers to the series of activities through which a company will attain its mission and vision. *Strategies* are the actions through which management will achieve the strategic goals. *Tactics* are the actions management intends to use to achieve the tactical goals. *Operations* are the actions management intends to use to achieve the operational goals.

Policies are statements that provide general guidance for decision-making in attaining a company's goals. Policies describe the context within which strategies, tactics, and operations are planned, implemented, and controlled.

Strategic, tactical, and operational goals are usually defined in terms of results or outcomes. Strategies, tactics, and operations are usually defined in terms of actions management will take to achieve the various goals. Figure 6-5 suggests possible criteria for operations goals.

Figure 6-5
Possible Criteria for Operational Goals

Objective Category	Performance Measurement	
Market Standing	a.	Market share
	b.	Total sales in dollars
	c.	Total sales in units
	d.	Total demand in units
Profitability	a.	Return on initial investment
	b.	Net profit
	c.	Earnings per share
	d.	Price/earnings ratio
	e.	Net profit/assets ratio
	f.	Net profit/sales ratio
	g.	Net profit/equity ratio
Productivity	a.	Total units produced
	b.	Unit production cost
	c.	Units produced per person-hour
	d.	Raw material required per unit
	e.	Sales/asset ratio
	f.	Inventory turnover ratio
	g.	Sales/plant and equipment book value ratio
Physical Resources	a.	Production workforce size
	b.	Raw material inventory
	c.	Finished goods inventory
	d.	Sales force size
Innovation	a.	Sales per salesperson
	b.	Productivity
Financial Resources	a.	Net current assets
	b.	Current ratio
	c.	Quick ratio
	d.	Bond or loan interest
	e.	Cash flow/net worth ratio
	f.	Bonds/equity ratio
	g.	Retained earnings
	h.	Dividends per share

The basic types of strategies that can be pursued by the management of BUSPOG companies include a *stability strategy*, a *growth strategy*, a *retrenchment strategy*, or some combination of the three.

Often, the officers of a simulated company explicitly adopt a *stability strategy* of maintaining market share while increasing profitability through better cost control. If this strategy is consistent with the goals previously delineated by the company's management, it may lead to successful results. There is a danger, however, associated with this strategy. In particular, the company must make sure that its level of activity for those decision variables that affect product demand is high enough to maintain its market share. If one of the company's competitors is pursuing a *growth strategy*, the level for such variables will, in all likelihood, have to be increased just to maintain a stable position.

BUSPOG companies also can pursue a *growth strategy* by outperforming competitors in the decision areas of Sales Price, Advertising, Sales Force, Product Research and Development, Sales Commission, Profit-Sharing, Sales Training, and Market-Share Increases. This strategy has at least one danger -- the company often will increase its market share but not recognize its profitability is decreasing . Some companies continue this disregard of profitability until they become financially insolvent.

In the BUSPOG world as in the real world, the *retrenchment strategy* would probably be adopted by Top Management only if the company is no longer capable of competing. This could result when the company does not have the human resources (either sales force or production work force) or financial resources necessary. (Lack of financial resources is the more frequently encountered cause of selecting the retrenchment strategy.) Under any of these conditions, Top management may choose to pursue a *retrenchment* strategy of scaling down its activities in one or more of the three markets.

Finally, a *combination strategy* might be adopted by Top Managment when the economic environment, the industrial environment, and the company's internal situation indicate a *growth strategy* would be successful; at other times they use a *stability strategy* unless a lack of resources indicates a *retrenchment strategy* is required.

In order to evaluate alternative strategies, Top Management should compare the predicted performance from each strategy with the performance goals of the company. Invariably this comparison involves assessing the profitability of each strategy, either explicitly or informally. As in the real world, profitability should be evaluated on the basis of the *degree of risk* involved, the *quality of the profits*, and the *timing of profit flows*.

Regardless of the strategy selected, Top Mmanagement of a BUSPOG company should define its organization's scope of operations. Will the company compete in all three markets? In only one? In both of the consumer markets? In only the industrial market? In one consumer market and the industrial market? This decision should be explicitly made and explicitly stated. This ensures that all involved will be aware of this aspect of the company's strategy and that the allocation of resources in all the functional areas will support the strategy.

Policies

In both the BUSPOG world, and the real world, the primary role of policies in implementing strategy is to improve the quality of decision-making. Accordingly, the areas where policies should be established are determined by the decisions to be made.

A BUSPOG company's management may wish to specify a policy for pricing relative to the remainder of the industry and/or a policy on the emphasis to be given to advertising versus the use of Salespersons, that is, a *marketing mix*. Management might establish a policy to help decide how to allocate funds between Product R & D and Process R & D. A policy in production capacity would assist management in making decisions on the Scheduled Production Work Week and the Production Workforce. Other policies could treat the problems of providing sufficient Raw Material and of distributing the Finished Product to the Three Markets. Employee compensation policies are helpful for determining Sales Salaries and Commissions, Production Wage Rates, and Profit-Sharing Levels. In like manner, a company policy regarding employee development is useful in setting the Sales and Production Training Budgets. Finally, a company's management may wish to establish policies governing the sources and uses of funds.

To gain a greater understanding of possible policies, study the list of policies presented in Figure 6-6. These are some of the policies that were specified in a recent player's report, and policies are stated in the student's own words. They are offered as examples rather than models to be emulated.

Figure 6-6
Examples of Policies.

1. The company will follow industry price trends only when its price is found to be 5 percent variant from the industry median. When such a condition is encountered, the company will alter its price to conform to the industry median if a profit sufficient to meet the financial objectives of the company can be made.
2. If the company's prices are within the limits established above, Price will be decreased by up to 50 percent of any cost reductions realized through Process R&D.
3. The company will hire at least one Salesperson per Market per quarter as long as the total Sales Force does not exceed fifty persons. Should the Sales Force drop below twenty-five persons, hiring will be eight persons per quarter (for all three markets) until a level of forty salespersons is realized.
4. Research and development expenditures will be increased at an average of 2 percent per quarter for both Product and Process R&D.
5. Expansion of Production capacity will be financed with at least 50 percent of the funds coming from Retained Earnings and with the balance coming from bonded indebtedness of the sale of Common Stock.
6. An increase in Sales Salaries will be made effective within Quarter 3 of each year. The amount of the increase will be linked to the increase in sales for the past four quarters and the sales for the prior four quarters. The amount of increase will follow this schedule:

Percent Increase in Sales	Sales Salary Increase
None or decrease	0
1 TO 5	$100
6 TO 10	$200
11 OR MORE	$300

7. Demand for increased production for six months or less will be met with overtime scheduling.
8. Demand for increased production in excess of six months will be met with an expansion of production capacity.
9. Advertising expenditures will be made in order to meet these criteria:

   Market 1: Company will maintain the highest advertising budget for this market.

   Market 2: Company will use the *average estimated* and *advertising levels* for the industry, by market,

   Market 3: for the prior quarter as the basis for establishing expenditure levels. The actual expenditure will fall within 20 percent of those amounts.

These policies would aid Top Management in making decisions regarding Common Stock, Bonds, Bank Loans, Savings Account Accumulations, and Dividends.

As previously stated, policies serve as guides to decision-making; they do not dictate specific decisions. The use of such guides results in more consistency, coordination, and integration of actions and plans within and across the functional areas. While decisions can be made by the-seat-of -the-pants method, this is usually less successful than an approach involving the consideration of explicitly-stated policies as guides .

Appraisal System

The final step in planning for effective decision-making is to establish an Appraisal System for *evaluating and controlling* the operations of a company. One characterization of the system required is given in Figure 6-7. This model includes the three elements common to all control systems: measurement of output, comparison to desired standards, and taking corrective action.

At each round of play, the Top Management Team provides values for the twenty decision variables. These, together with the influences from the Economic Environment and the Task Environment, are combined in the BUSPOG computer program. The results are presented in the six sections of the Output Report which are roughly equivalent to the results a company in the real world obtains from ongoing operations.

The officers of each BUSPOG company should extract values from the Output Report for those performance measures they believe are necessary to properly appraise the effectiveness of their strategies, tactics, and operations. Figure 6-5 lists a number of measures that may be useful in the BUSPOG competition.

There are two schools of thought in the management literature on *strategic planning* which relate to appraising the performance of a company. One school recommends standards that come from considerations of what constitutes effective company operations — adequate profit, market share, etc., this school compare results from operations against these standards.

The second school of thought is, if you do an adequate job of goal-setting, you have already identified the standards against which you should compare the results of your operations. Earlier in the chapter much was said about setting *operational goals*. These goals, it seems, are the most appropriate standards to use in appraising results and adjusting actions to improve them.

Any differences found between what you want to achieve (your goals) and what you are achieving (your results) should be analyzed to find out if the goals are achievable or unachievable. If it is determined that a goal you adopted is achievable within the scope of present operations, decisions should be adjusted to improve current operations. If it is determined the goal you adopted is now seen to be invalid (information available shows it is either unachievable or has already been achieved), then this information must be brought to the attention of the management that set the goal. In either case management must make changes in its operating decisions or its mission and vision, goals, strategies, tactics, operations, and/or policies in order to maximize their positive effects.

Figure 6-7
Appraisal System

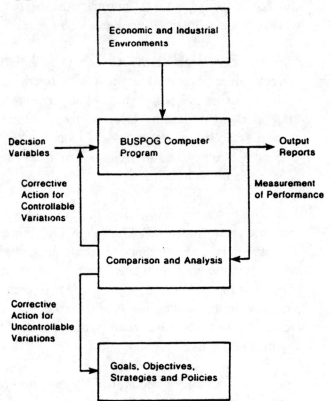

Of paramount importance in the real world is an organization's information system . It is the same in BUSPOG. Although all of the competing companies receive the same type of information, some management teams will use it to better advantage than others. Some teams use the data from the Output Report as inputs to their Appraisal System. Other teams view the data from the reports as ends unto themselves. Such a team is using a play-it-by-ear approach to the BUSPOG competition and not attempting a formal appraisal of its company's performance. Needless to say, - those teams which use a formal Appraisal System seem not only to fare better in the competition but also to learn more from the BUSPOG experience.

Marketing Management

7

As is true for most real world industrial organizations, the Marketing function in BUSPOG (see Figure 2-2) is the primary informational link with the customers. In the game, this link is created through five decisions:

1. Selling Price in each of the Three Markets
2. Advertising budget for each of the Three Markets
3. Salespersons hired or discharged in each of the Three Markets
4. Product Research and Development Budget for the company
5. Sales Commissions for the company

In addition to handling these decision-making responsibilities, the Marketing Vice-President of a company provides Sales Forecasts. This function is critical because these projections serve as the basis for planning in all the other functions of the organization.

Effects of Marketing Variables

The simulated market potential of the game is responsive to variables within the Economic Environment, the Task Environment, the Marketing function, and the Human Resources Function. In order to formulate viable strategies and policies, the Top Management Team of each company needs to estimate the form and the level of the responsiveness (or *elasticity*) for each of the variables. The predictability of the underlying demand pattern as a function of time must be ascertained. That is, the demand pattern must be determined as trending, seasonal, cyclic, and/or irregular in

nature. Determination of this nature of time facilitates prediction of Product Demand and Sales.

The general relationship of many of the variables within the game model takes the form of what is termed a Growth Curve as shown in Figure 7-1. The growth-curve relationship has a *minimum effect* level, which is indicated as A in figure 7-1. If the *value* for the variable is at a level of B or less, the effect of the variable is at the minimum level A. As the value of the variable is made larger than B, the effect of the variable increases according to the Growth Curve until a *maximum effect* level of C is attained. If the value

Figure 7-1
Growth Curve Relationship

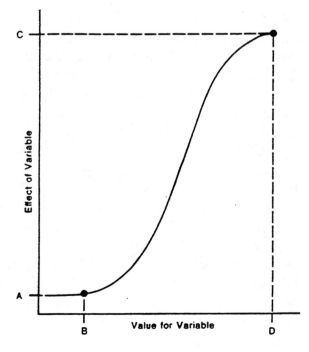

for any variable becomes greater than D, the effect of the variable remains unchanged at its maximum value C. Thus, a general characterization of this model is that low variable values have very little effect since there is a *threshold* or minimum value of the variable necessary to obtain an increase in the effect. After the threshold value has been achieved, an increase in the variable has an increased effect until a saturation or *maximum effect value* is attained. Increases in the variable above the saturation value are wasted since no corresponding increased effect is achieved.

In addition, the relationships depicted by the model include the possibility that the effects of variables may be felt in more than one time period. For example, the effect of Advertising expenditures made during a particular quarter of the year may not only influence the Product Demand in that quarter but also in the next quarter and perhaps in later quarters. This lag in response is more pronounced for some variables than for others.

The effect on demand of the five marketing variables -- (1) Sales Price Levels, (2) Advertising Expenditures, (3) Size of Sales Force, (4) Product Research and Development Expenditures, and (5) Sales Commission Levels -- has the Lagged--Response and Growth Curve Relationships of Figure 7-1.

As price is decreased, the *sales appeal* of a company's products is increased; that is, the demand for the company's products is increased. Similarly, as the advertising expenditures and/or sales force sizes are increased, the market responds with an increase in demand. Resources allocated to product research and development can result in technological changes in the product, which in turn are reflected in a greater sales appeal of the product. Finally, an increase in the sales commission paid by a company results in a greater effort by the sales force, which may show up as an increased demand. Each of these variables also has a cost. A decision to increase or decrease these and other costs must be based on a consideration of the value of change which will result from the investment and the cost of the investment. This comparison is frequently made into a ratio with the benefit on top and the cost on the bottom. Assuming the investment can be financed, any investment over 1.0 should be undertaken.

In addition, two of the variables within the Human Resources function have an effect on product demand. One is the level of expenditures for Sales Training and the other is the level of employee Profit Sharing. The hypothesis is that as the Sales Training Budget is increased, the sales force will be more skillful in promoting the company's products and sales will increase. In a similar vein, as the level of employee Profit-Sharing is increased, the Salespersons find it to their direct benefit to be more effective. Since both Salespeople and Production Workers participate in Profit-Sharing, investments in this area motivate both groups .

Marketing Planning Procedure

Designing a marketing plan is the first step in planning, implementing, and controlling a procedure to achieve the selected strategic, tactical, and operational goals and to conform to adopted policies.

Marketing Plan

The vice president in charge of the marketing function should come to each decision-making session ready to recommend a set of marketing decisions for the next time period. After a thorough discussion, the rest of the management team either accepts the officer's recommendations for the five marketing decisions or modifies them. An example of a BUSPOG form for facilitating a three-year marketing plan is shown in Figure 6-3. (Similar blank forms are in Appendix B.)

The Marketing Vice-President must interact closely with all members of the company team. In reality, the interaction will probably be greater than what has been suggested at this point. For example, if production determines that the com-

52

pany cannot produce all the product desired by marketing, the marketing plan may need to be reworked. Also, financial management may determine that the marketing plan could place the company in a financially unsound position. Insuring integration and coordination is one of the major responsibilities of the president of the company.

To aid in our discussion, Table 7-1 has been partially completed as though decisions are being made for Year 2 Quarter 2 from the historical data presented in Appendix A. Information is presented for additional years to demonstrate one way to insure the continuity of planning activity. BUSPOG teams may choose not to adopt this practice, especially at the beginning of play, because the value of the practice may prove less than the time it requires. It is quite helpful, however, to adopt extended planning activities as soon as possible.

Remember you are in Year 2, Quarter 2, and the data in this form is accurate for Quarter 1 and Quarter 2; later quarters and especially later years may or may not prove true. When planning future actions, managers frequently use an approach called *rolling planning*. A plan is made for a complete time period (in this case, the next three years); then the first segment (the next year) is planned using the next shorter time segments (quarters). As each quarter is experienced, the real numbers are substituted for the planned numbers. Plans are then modified to do either more or less, and goals are modified to reflect any altered reality.

According to **Line 1** of Table 7-1, this company is planning to maintain its price in Market 1 during Year 2 then raise it slightly, in years 3 and 4. On the other hand, **Line 2** shows that the company intends to steadily raise the price in Market 2 throughout Years 2, 3, and 4 but encourages sales in Quarters 1 and 4 by dropping price because of fluctuations in seasonal demand. For Market 3, the company plans slight price increases as indicated on **Line 3** during Year 2 but will drop prices once they have developed a stronger sales force.

Line 4 of Table 7-1 suggests that this company

intends to try to increase its sales in Market 1 by a steady increase in advertising expenditures. (The amounts given on Line 4 are quarterly expenditures for the first year and yearly amounts for the remaining two years. This is also true for lines 5 through 10 and lines 12 through 19 of this form.)

The advertising expenditures on lines 5 and 6 for Markets 2 and 3 are not all filled in. The reader may wish to add his or her own numbers in the blank spaces as preparation for using such a form later.

After the advertising expenditures have been determined, the next step is to decide on the sales force level. The treatment of this decision differs in that the marketing and human resources officers must work together on it. First, the marketing vice president decides on a desired sales force for each of the three markets for the next three years. These are given to the human resources vice-president who in turn uses them as inputs for a Human Resources Plan. An example of a human resources plan is shown in Table 9-1. Lines 5, 11, and 17 of Table 9-1 show the size of the sales force desired by the marketing vice president for each of the three markets. One result the human resources vice president subsequently obtains from the human resources plan is the change in the number of salespersons for each market. These are shown on lines 6, 12, and 18 on the human resources plan and are transferred to Lines 7, 8, and 9 on the Marketing plan. On both the Marketing Plan and the Human Resources Plan, the hiring of salespersons is denoted by positive numbers, and the discharging of salespersons is denoted by negative numbers. The player may wish to complete these sales force entries in Table 7-1 for practice.

The final two decisions of the marketing vice president are on the expenditures for Product Research and Development (R&D) (**Line 10**) and the Sales Commission level (**Line 11**). According to Table 7-1, this company intends to steadily increase its Product R & D budget but does not contemplate changing its 0.3 percent Sales Com-

Table 7-1
Marketing Plan Form

		Year 2				Year 3	Year 4
	Marketing Decisions	Qtr. 1	Qtr. 2	Qtr. 3	Qtr. 4		
1	Product Price - Mkt. 1 (in dollars)						
2	Product Price - Mkt. 2						
3	Product Price - Mkt. 3						
4	Advertising - Mkt.1 (in thousands of dollars)						
5	Advertising - Mkt.2						
6	Advertising - Mkt.3						
7	Salespersons - Mkt. 1						
8	Salespersons - Mkt. 2						
9	Salespersons - Mkt. 3						
10	Product R & D (in thousands of dollars)						
11	Sales Commission (in percent)						
Forecasted Sales							
12	Sales in - Market 1 Units						
13	Market 2						
14	Market 3						
15	Total						
16	Sales in Market 1 Dollars						
17	Market 2						
18	Market 3						
19	Total						

mission over the next three years

As was previously pointed out, one of the extremely important responsibilities of the marketing function is to provide the best possible forecast of the number of units which will be sold in each market in order that the production function can develop a production plan. In addition, a sales forecast in terms of dollars is needed by the finance function in order to develop the financial plans. **Lines 12 through 15** present the Unit Sales Forecast for the individual markets and the Total for all three. **Lines 16 through 19** show the Sales in dollars for the individual markets and the Total Sales for all three. It hardly seems necessary to note that sales in dollars are the product of Sales in units times the Price in dollars for each market.

Sales Forecast Form

The sales projections on **Lines 12 through 19** of Table 7-1 can be developed in a number of ways: expert opinion, forecasting techniques such as exponential smoothing or linear regression based on historical experience, extrapolations of line graphs of sales for each quarter, causality, or even unfounded guesses. The most important consideration is that a number of forecasting methods (the more the better) and the method which generates the best forecast (the least error between the forecast and the experienced demand) be used. It is also necessary to continue checking the error between forecast and demand since that is the only way to identify when something has changed.

A BUSPOG form for combining expert opinion (the judgment of the vice-president of marketing) and some quantitative techniques to forecast demand is illustrated in Table 7-2. (Blank copies of this form are provided in Appendix B.) The game administrator may require the use of this approach for sales forecasting or may allow some other approach.

Turn now to Table 7-2 . Like the Marketing Plan Form, the Sales Forecast Form is laid out to accommodate a three-year plan. Notice that one of these forms is to be completed for each of the three markets. The first two items to be entered on the form are the sales and the demand for the previous quarter. Values for these are found in the Production and Sales Output Report (Section 2) of the previous quarter. Both Previous Quarter Sales and Previous Quarter Demand are in terms of the number of units of finished product and are entered on **Lines 1 and 2** in the column for the Quarter for which the form is being prepared (in this case, Year 2, Quarter 2).

At this point, let us review why demand and sales may not be equal. If the figure for demand is greater than the figure for sales, the company has sold more of its product than it was able to supply. In other words, the company ran out of finished product in that sales district. In the BUSPOG program when this happens, 50 percent of the unfilled orders become backorders, the other 50 percent are filled by competitors who have sufficient stock to meet the additional demand. The allocations to the competitors are made in proportion to how well each company is competing based on the five marketing and two human resources variables previously discussed. On the other hand, if sales are greater than the forecasted demand, the company has gained in sales because at least one of its competitors has not been able to fill all of its orders in this market. Additional customers obtained in this manner generally remain as customers in future periods.

The next 15 lines of the Sales Forecast Form estimate changes to the previous period's demand due to changes which may have occurred in both the external environment and the internal situation. **Lines 3 and 4** allow for adjustments resulting from a stockout situation. **Line 3** is used to reflect the loss or gain of customers due to stockouts. If another company incurs a stockout, some of its disappointed customers will be permanently lost by the company and gained by you and the other competitors who supplied the products. If Previous Quarter Sales are more than Previous Quarter Demand, the difference is a permanent

Table 7-2
Sales Forecast Form
Market _____
(figures expressed in units)

		Year ____				Year ____	Year ____
		Qtr. 1	Qtr. 2	Qtr. 3	Qtr. 4	Total	Total
1	Previous Quarter Sales						
2	Previous Quarter Demand						
3	Customer Change						
4	Backorders						
5	Trend						
6	Seasonal						
7	Gross Domestic Prod.						
8	Pers. Consump. Exp.						
9	Household Forma.						
10	Price						
11	Advertising						
12	Sales Force Chg.						
13	Product R & D						
14	Sales Commission						
15	Sales Training						
16	Profit Sharing						
17	Total Adjustments						
18	Forecasted Demand						
19	Stockout Effect						
20	Forecasted Sales						

gain in your customer base. On the other hand, if it is your company whose Previous Quarter Demand is more than Previous Quarter Sales, it is your customer base that is reduced by this difference.

Line 4 is for entering estimated Back Orders from one quarter to the next. If Previous Quarter Demand and Previous Quarter Sales are the same, there is no increase or decrease in demand caused by changes in the customer base or backorders. In the historical record provided in Appendix A, Sales are equal to Demand. During actual play, this will not always be the case.

The next two lines facilitate changes due to fluctuations in the underlying demand pattern. **Line 5** is used for anticipated changes in the overall trend in Demand. Values for this entry can be positive or negative although the trend has been slightly positive (perhaps 1 percent a year in recent years). You can track the trend from your historical data if you will plot time on your X axis against demand on your Y axis.

Line 6 allows adjustment for any Seasonal Effect on Sales. Unless the game administrator indicates otherwise, sales can be expected to be highest in Quarters 2 and 3. To be more accurate in your forecast of seasonality, check any standard quantitative methods text (preferably one with a related software package) which addresses Time Series. Focus on the parts which describe how to calculate and use seasonal indexes.

In **Lines 7, 8, and 9** you will adjust your forecast for anticipated changes in the three economic variables: (1) Gross Domestic Product (**Line 7**); (2) Personal Consumption Expenditures for Durable Goods (**Line 8**); and (3) Number of Household Formations (**Line 9**). All of these may have a direct effect on Demand; that is, as these variables increase in value, so does Product Demand. In making this estimate, it is probably easiest to guess how much a particular change in one of these variables will cause a change in demand.

As an example, the Number of Household Formations predicted for Year 2 Quarter 2 is 386,000. How many of these new households are in Market 1? How many of them will buy a videocassette recorder during Year 2, Quarter 3? What part of that increase in the market for videocassette recorders will your company capture? That estimate should be entered on **Line 9** of the Sales Forecast Form for Year 2, Quarter 3. Similar estimates should be made and entered for **Line 7** (Gross Domestic Product) and **Line 8** (Personal Consumption Expenditures).

Will you be making any changes in the five marketing variables discussed earlier in this chapter or the two human Resources variables that affect demand (Sales Training Expenditures and Profit Sharing)? **Lines 10 through 16** record adjustments to demand due to the new decisions.
The effect on demand of the Human Resource decisions are discussed in Chapter 9.

The values on **Lines 3 through 16** are totaled to determine Total Adjustment, which is entered on **Line 17.**

The value of Total Adjustment (**Line 17**) is added to the value of Previous Quarter Demand (**Line 2**) to determine the Forecasted Demand which is recorded on **Line 8**.

Forecasted Sales (**Line 20**) is calculated from Forecasted Demand, (**Line 18**) and contains whatever stockout effect, if any, is anticipated during the quarter. If you anticipate a stockout for your company, the entry on **Line 19** is negative and the amount is the estimated number of

resulting lost sales. If you anticipate a competitor's stockout, the **Line 19** entry is positive and is the number of sales you estimate you will gain.

The values on Lines 18 and 19 are totaled to yield the Forecasted Sales on **Line 20.**

This entire process is repeated for Market 2 and for Market 3. If you are planning for a three-year period, the values from Lines 18 and 20 in the last quarter are carried forward to Lines 1 and 2 for then next quarter.

The values given on Line 20 for each market are transferred to Lines 12, 13, and 14 of the Marketing Plan Form (Table 7-1) in the column corresponding to that time period.

To repeat, as long as you are using this approach to forecasting the next quarter's demand, a Sales Forecast Form should be completed for each market in which the company is competing.

Summary

The procedure for making marketing decisions includes these steps:

1. Select the Price and Advertising levels for each of the Three Markets.

2. Select Sales Force Size for all Three Markets and forward them to Human Resources Management.

3. Obtain Sales Force changes for All Three Markets from the Human Resources Plan. Enter on the Marketing Plan.

4. Select Product Research and Development and Sales Commission levels for the company.

5. Forward all changes in the five Marketing decision-variables to Financial management and the President.

6. Obtain last period's Demand and Sales values for each of the Three Markets from the Production and Sales, Section 2, of the Output Report.

7. Estimate the fourteen adjustments to Demand for each of the Three Markets.

8. For each of the Three Markets, compute Forecasts for Demand and Sales in units and Sales Revenue in dollars.

9. Transfer the three forecasts of sales in units and the three forecasts of sales in dollars to the Marketing Plan and find the Total Unit and Total Dollar Sales Values.

10. Forward the unit sales data to Production Management. Forward both the Unit and Dollar Sales data to Financial Management and the President.

Production Management

8

Production is that portion of the organization depicted in Overall Organizational Operations (Figure 2-1) that is concerned with transforming Raw Materials and the efforts of the Production Workforce into Finished Products which are ready to sell. The Number of Units of Finished Products and their distribution to the Three Markets are based on the Sales Forecast provided by the Marketing Department.

Level of production is restricted by the production capacity of the factory (largely determined by the size of the production work force and the length of their workweek since BUSPOG adjusts plant and equipment to a size appropriate to the size of the workforce) and the amount of raw material available at the time. Planning and scheduling the size of the Production Workforce, Production Hours, raw Material Inventories, and Allocation of newly produced videocassette recorders and are all vital responsibilities of Production Management.

The particular decisions to be made every quarter by the Production Function include:

1. Production Scheduled (hours/week)
2. Labor Force Change (number of workers)
3. Allocation to Markets (%)
4. Process R&D ($1000/qtr.)
5. Raw Materials Ordered (million lbs.)

Effects of Production Variables

The effect of most of the production variables is more certain than that of the marketing variables discussed in the previous chapter. In this respect the game reflects the situation found in many if not most real-world industrial organizations.

The Production Output of a company is equal to the Total Scheduled Production Hours in the quarter times the size of the Production Labor Force times the Productivity.

The Total Scheduled Production Hours are the number of hours the Production Workforce is scheduled to work each week (the Production Scheduled (hours/week)) times the number of weeks in a quarter (13). This production factor is known, then, with considerable certainty.

The size of the Production Labor Force is controlled by the second production decision (Labor Force Change). Because there is a possibility of *voluntary terminations* (which will be discussed in the next chapter) the size of the Production Labor Force is not completely determined by a company's management.

In the real world, Productivity is largely a function of the manufacturing technology being used, the skill of the production workers, and the worker's motivation. These three variables also affect Productivity in BUSPOG:

1. Since expenditures on Process Research and Development improve the company's production technology, Productivity increases as the level of this expenditure increases.

2. As the expenditures on Production Training increase, Productivity will increase since it is assumed this expenditure increases the job skills of the Production Work Force.

3. In like manner, an increase in the level of Profit-Sharing with employees will motivate

the production Labor Force to become more productive.

In addition, there may be some small random variations in Productivity from quarter to quarter.

Productivity per person-hour is one of the production factors that has the growth curve and lagged-response effect (discussed in the previous chapter with Figure 7-1).

The Raw Material Required (pounds of raw material required for each finished product) is assumed to be affected by the same three variables but in an inverse manner. Namely, an increase in Process Research and Development expenditures usually results in improved raw material technology with a corresponding decrease in the raw material required. An increase in a company's Production Training budget or employee Profit-Sharing level will decrease the Raw Material Required (workers waste less material). Again, there may be small random variations in the Raw Material Requirements.

Production Planning Procedure

The Sales Forecast is the foundation for Production, Human Resources, and Financial planning. Using the Sales Forecast, the Production Vice-President must schedule enough production and allocate it appropriately to the different markets in order to satisfy the forecasted demand. If management does not succeed in this, the company will run out of finished products to sell to potential customers. When this happens, some of the unfilled orders are carried to the next quarter in the form of back orders. The remaining customers buy from competitors. Not all of the unsatisfied customers will return to the company in the future. Therefore, careful production planning is one key to maintaining a company's clientele.

Production Plan

Availability of production resources is not a

limited in the operating environment of BUSPOG. There is no physical restriction on the availability of production capacity, labor supply, or raw materials for a company. Sufficient financial resources, however, must be available to purchase these resources. The Cost of Production, therefore, is a very important consideration when formulating an effective Production Plan; it must be coordinated carefully with the Financial Plan.

Figure 8-1

Production's Response to Seasonality of Demand

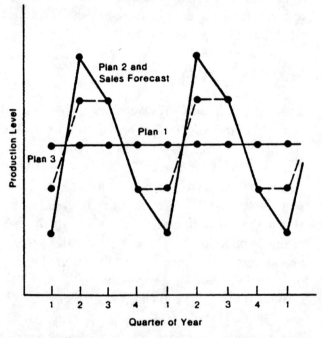

An important consideration when planning your production is the trade-off in Cost of continually changing production output to meet a changing Sales pattern as opposed to maintaining a constant production output. One way to adjust your production output to meet the sales pattern is to adjust the size of your Poduction Workforce by hiring and firing production workers as necessary. Each time you hire or fire an employee, however, you incur a cost. Another way to change your production output to meet a changing sales pattern is to change the number of hours you ask production employees to work each week. In accordance with the Fair Labor Standards Act, the standard work week is 40 hours. If you ask your nonexempt employees (those who are not exempt from the requirements of the Fair Labor Standards Act) to work more than 40 hours a week, you must pay them 150% of their usual hourly wage. In BUSPOG there is an absolute maximum of 60 hours a week which allows only 20 hours of overtime. Also assume previous management negotiated a contract with your production workers' labor union that requires you to pay them for 40 hours a week even when they work less.

An alternative approach to designing a Production Plan in response to your anticipated pattern of demand would be to forecast the average Demand for the year and to adjust the size of your Production Workforce and Scheduled workweek to produce the Average Demand. In quarters when demand is below your level of production, the surplus would be carried over as Finished Product Inventory. In quarters when demand is above your level of production, the shortfall would come out of the inventory.

The main problem with this approach is that a storage cost is incurred at the end of the quarter for each unit in the Finished Product Inventory that is carried forward to the next quarter.

Therefore, the financial concerns may be the chief criteria in deciding which production policy to follow, especially as your ability to evaluate complex outcomes grows.

For example, suppose the forecasted two-year demand is as shown by the heaviest solid line of Figure 8-1. A constant Production Plan is shown as Plan 1. In Quarters 1 and 4 of this plan, Production would be greater than demand, with the excess carried as inventory to be sold in Quarters 2 and 3. Since there is almost always a cost associated with carrying an inventory, a Production Plan which maintains a constant level of production (such as this) would incur considerably higher Finished Product Inventory storage cost than other plans.

Plan 2 of Figure 8-1 keeps production equal to the Sales Forecast for each quarter. Inventory storage costs would be less for this plan, but it has other costs, not in Plan 1, which are associated with changes in production output. Changes in production output are made by varying the number of workers or by using overtime. Either approach has costs associated with it. Plan 2, then with four changes each year, would have either high - worker-change costs or high overtime costs.

Plan 3 is a compromise between the other two plans. Production for two quarters each year is greater than Sales (as in Plan 1), and there are two changes each year in the production costs (as in Plan 2). This plan may have lower costs than either of the previous plans. Obviously, the preferable plan must be identified through careful calculations.

To assist players in their production planning efforts, a Production Plan Form is provided in Table 8-1.

The first entries on this form are the Sales Forecasts for each of the Three Markets. These can be obtained from **Lines 12, 13, and 14** of the Marketing Plan (Table 7-1) or from line 20 of the Sales Forecast Form (Table 7-2) for each of the Three Markets. These entries are entered on **Lines 1, 5, and 9** of Table 8-1.

Once you build a spreadsheet to support your decision-making, you can link these two sheets so that the input for the Production Plan comes automatically when you enter Forecasted Demand into your Marketing Plan.

The Desired Ending Inventory at the end of the quarter should be entered for the three markets on **Lines 2, 6, and 10**. The size of this inventory should be chosen strictly on the basis of inventory policy. (One policy might be to maintain a minimum of 10,000 units in Finished Product Inventory. Another might be that the desired inventory at the end of the quarter 1 be a percentage of the forecasted demand.)

Table 8-1
Production Plan Form
(Figures expressed in units)

			Year 2				Year 3	Year 4
			Qtr. 1	Qtr. 2	Qtr. 3	Qtr. 4		
1	Market 1	Sales Forecast						
2		Desired End Inventory						
3		Beginning Inventory						
4		Production Required						
5	Market 2	Sales Forecast						
6		Desired End Inventory						
7		Beginning Inventory						
8		Production Required						
9	Market 3	Sales Forecast						
10		Desired End Inventory						
11		Beginning Inventory						
12		Production Required						
13	**Total**	Production Required						
14		Productivity						
15		Hours Scheduled						
16		Prod. Force Required (number of persons)						
17		Prod. Force Change (number of persons)						
18	**Market 1 Allocation** (percentage)							
19	**Market 2 Allocation** (percentage)							
20	**Market 3 Allocation** (percentage)							

The policy concerning the size of Desired Inventory at the end of the quarter should be set after a consideration of:

- costs for the production, overtime, and storage involved
- the contribution to profit which will be gained from each additional sale (the difference between the cost of making a new product and the price at which the sale is made)
- the size of the error between your forecast of demand and the actual demand
- the amount of safety stock (Finished Product) you desire, assuming your contribution to profit is a lot higher than the cost of storing an additional unit.

The inventory at the end of the last quarter of play is the same as the beginning inventory of the next quarter. Its values (which can be found in the Production and Sales Section of the Output Report), are entered on **Lines 3, 7, and 11** of the production plan. The production required for **Lines 4, 8, and 12** is then computed in this way:

Production Required = Sales Forecast
   + Desired Ending Inventory
   - Beginning Inventory

The sum of the values on Lines 4, 8, and 12 is the Total Production Required and is entered on **Line 13**. The value for the Productivity for the last quarter (Line 14) is found on the Production and Sales Section of the Output Report. This value can be used as the basis for forecasting the next quarter's productivity value and is entered on **Line 14**.

The next entry will be easier to understand if, before proceeding, we review. A *tradeoff* must be considered when deciding how many workers will be needed and how many hours each should work per week. Fewer production workers require more hours to produce a given amount of finished goods. Conversely, more workers will require fewer hours to produce the same number of goods. Consider these relationships:

Total Production per quarter =
   (Production Hours Scheduled)(Productivity)

Production Hours Scheduled =
   (Production hours per week)(number of weeks per quarter)(number of Production Workers).

Combining these two,

Total Production per quarter =
   (Production hours per week)(weeks per quarter)(number of Production Workers)(Productivity)

If you change the number of production workers, the number of production hours scheduled for each week will change. If you change the number of production hours scheduled for each week, the number of production workers will change.

Here is one procedure for completing Table 8-1. The Hours Scheduled **(Line 15)** are found by multiplying the number of Production Hours Scheduled per week times the number of weeks in a quarter (13). The number of production hours per week may be any value between zero and sixty. However, if the work week is less than forty hours, the company's labor contract requires that the production work force be paid for forty hours. Also, if it is greater than forty hours per week, an overtime rate of 150 percent of the regular labor rate is paid for all hours worked over forty hours.

The value for the Production Force Required **(Line 16)** is found by dividing the Total Production required on **Line 13** by the Productivity on **Line 14**. The result is then divided by the Hours Scheduled on **Line 15**.

Conversely, the value for the hours Scheduled on **Line 15** can be found by dividing the Total Production Required by the value for Productivity and also by the value for the Desired Production Labor Force. If you are using a spreadsheet, this calculation becomes very simple because the Production Force Required will be recalculated automatically when you change the number of Hours Scheduled.

The Production and Human Resources officers must work together to determine the value for

Production Force Change (**Line 17**). The Production Force Required (Line 16) is given to the human resources Vice-President for use as one of the inputs into the Human Resources Plan. (Table 9-1 in the next chapter presents an example of a Human Resources Plan.)

Line 22 in Table 9-1 shows the Production Force Desired which has been taken from Line 16 of the Production Plan Form. When the Adjusted Size (**Line 21**) is subtracted from Production Force Desired (**Line 22**), **Line 23** indicates the required Change in the labor force. The value from Line 23 in the Human Resources Plan is transferred to Line 17 of the Production Plan (Table 8-1) and is also transferred to the Quarterly Decision Sheet.

Since persons can be hired or discharged from the production labor force, a positive number corresponds to an increase in the labor force and a negative number to a decrease.

The BUSPOG program recognizes that changes in the Production Workforce require corresponding changes to be made in the company's Plant and Equipment capacity. Such changes are made automatically by the program. Consequently, an increase in the labor force results in an investment in plant and equipment. Conversely, a decrease in the labor force results in some inflow of cash from the sale of plant and equipment assets.

In the Production Plan (Table 8-1) the Allocations of Finished Product to the Three Markets on **Lines 18, 19, and 20** are found by taking the values of Lines 4, 8, and 12 and dividing each by the value of Line 13 then multiplying these results by 100 to convert them to percentages. The Allocation of Finished Product to the Three Markets is an especially important consideration in BUSPOG since the game does not allow a later transfer of product from one warehouse to another. These allocation figures become the figures you enter in your decisions.

Raw Material Plan

A company must insure that it has enough raw material available to meet its Production Plan. This requires checking to insure you have enough

raw material for the present quarter and at least the next quarter because the delivery time for raw material is one quarter (three months). For example, the raw material you order in Quarter 2 year cannot be used for production until Quarter 3.

If a company has less raw material than necessary for scheduled production, it can only produce until its raw material is used up. This makes it very desirable to have a little more raw material than what is required to meet the planned production. Of course, too much would waste money on storage costs.

Table 8-2 is an example of the BUSPOG Raw Material Plan Form. The value for Total Production Required on **Line 1** of this form is taken from **Line 13** of the Production Plan Form. The next item is the amount of Raw Material Required per Unit of Finished Product. Last quarter's value for this variable can be found in the Production and Sales Section of last quarter's Output Report. The value for this next quarter must be forecasted, based on last quarter's value, and entered on **Line 2**.

To determine the Raw Material Required (**Line 3**), multiply the value on Line 1 by the value on Line 2 and then divide by 1,000,000 to convert it to millions of pounds of raw material. The Beginning Raw Material Inventory (**Line 4**) is the same as the Ending Raw Material Inventory reported in the Production and Sales section of the Output Report.

Raw Material Remaining after Production (**Line 5**) is obtained by subtracting Raw Material Required (Line 3) from Beginning Raw Material Inventory (Line 4). It should be noted that this number, like all inventories, cannot be negative. If a negative result occurs, it means that you do not have enough Raw Material to produce the units indicated in Total Production Required (Line 1). This will require readjusting your Production Plan (Table 8-1) until Raw Material Remaining after Production (Line 5) is no longer negative.

Lines 6 and 7 of this form are used to calculate the Raw Material Inventory for future quarters when no output report is available. **Line 6** is the result

Table 8-2
Raw Material Plan Form

		Year 2				Year 3	Year 4
		Qtr. 1	Qtr. 2	Qtr. 3	Qtr. 4		
1	Total Production Required (in units)						
2	Raw Material Required per unit (in lbs./unit)						
3	Raw Material Required (in millions of lbs.)						
4	Beginning Raw Material Inventory (millions)						
5	Raw Material Remaining After Production (millions)						
6	Raw Material Required Next Period (millions)						
7	Desired Ending Inventory Next Period (millions)						
8	Raw Material to Order This Period (millions)						
9	Process R. & D.						

of multiplying (the forecasted demand for next quarter for all three markets) times (the expected raw material required per unit next quarter); again the result is converted to millions of pounds.

Line 7 is the Desired Ending Inventory for next quarter. Raw Material to Order **(Line 8)** is Raw Material Required Next period (Line 6) plus Desired Ending Inventory Next Period (Line 7) minus Raw Material Remaining After Production (Line 5).

The final step in completing the Raw Material Plan Form is the budget allocation to **Process Research and Development (Line 9)**. There is no significance in the fact that it is shown on the raw material plan.

Summary

The procedure for Production Management Decision-Making includes these steps:

1. Enter the Sales Forecast obtained from Marketing for all Three Markets on the Production Plan.
2. Select the desired levels for Finished Product Inventory for all Three Markets on the Production Plan.
3. Obtain the current Total Finished Product Inventory values from the Production and Sales section of the last Output Report.
4. Calculate the Production Required for each market and for the entire company.
5. Estimate future Productivity based on the current value reported in the Production and

Sales section of the last Output Report.

6. Select the values for the Hours of Scheduled Production and compute the Production Force Required or select values for the Production Force Required and compute the Hours of Scheduled Production .

7. Forward the size of the Production Labor force to personnel management and obtain the required change in the labor force from personnel.

8. Compute the Allocation of Production to the three markets.

9. Estimate future values for Raw Material per Unit based on the current value from the Production and Sales section of the Output Report and calculate the amount of Raw Material Required for Production.

10 From the Output Report, obtain the Beginning Raw Material Inventory value, which includes the Raw Material on Order, and calculate Raw Material Remaining After Production.

11. Based on Forecasted Demand for next period, estimate Raw Material Required Next Period.

12. Select the Desired Ending Raw Material Inventory Next Period.

13. Calculate the amount of Raw Material to Be Ordered, based on the Raw Material Required Next Period, Desired Ending Inventory Next Period, and Raw Material Remaining After Production.

14. Select values for Process Research and Development Expenditures.

15. Forward all changes in the five production decision variables and the predicted inventory levels for Finished Product and Raw Material to Financial Management and the President.

Human Resources Management

9

In the real world, the Human Resources Function is primarily concerned with recruiting, selecting, developing, utilizing, and accommodating the human resources of an organization. Questions about the practice of management and the effectiveness of the management team are generally the responsibility of top management and their specialized staffs.

In academically-based programs on the other hand, the study of the management of human resources management theory and organization behavior are usually housed in the same academic department. The introductory courses offered by this department cover all three.

If BUSPOG is to provide a capstone experience, especially for those involved in academic programs, must address all three areas: human Resources, management theory, and organization behavior.

Fortunately, BUSPOG simulates all three areas quite adequately. The study of human resources management is directly reflected in the five Human Resource Decisions and is discussed in depth in this chapter. Improving the practice of management was addressed in Chapter 6, Managing Your Growth. In addition to the discussions of motivating both the Salesforce and Production Workforce, the simulated management teams provide an opportunity to practice *emergent leadership, participative decision-making, disciplining employees,* and many other theories presented in most classes in organizational behavior.

Human Resources Management

As was previously indicated in Figure 2-1 and in Chapters 7 and 8, the BUSPOG Human Resources Vice-President is responsible not only for establishing a Human Resources Plan and for staffing the Sales and Production functions but also for the wage, salary, and training aspects of a company.

In particular, the Vice-President of Human Resources must be prepared to recommend and defend these five decisions each quarter:

1. Sales Salaries
2. Sales Training Budget
3. Production Wage Rate
4. Production Training Budget
5. Profit-Sharing

Effects of Human Resources Variables

In Chapter 7 it was noted you can, in addition to optimizing price, advertising, and number of sales people, also influence the demand for your product by increasing the *effectiveness* of your Sales Force. This is done by improving: the technology involved in your product (Product R & D), the selling skill of your sales force (Sales Training), and the motivation of your sales force (Sales Commission and Profit-Sharing). Two of these variables (Product R&D and Sales Commission) are Marketing decisions and two of them (Sales Training and Profit Sharing) are decisions of Human Resource Management. If all decisions which require the concurrence of the

Top Management Team are based on a thorough discussion of the recommendations of the functional specialists, this split of responsibility should prove no problem.

The effect of both of these Human Resource Variables -- Sales Training and Profit-Sharing -- has the form of a growth curve and lagged--response as discussed in conjunction with Figure 3-1.

In a similar manner, as discussed in Chapter 8, there are three aspects of Productivity: the technology used in the production process, the skill of the production workers, and the motivation of the production workers. The technology of production is enhanced by investments in Process R&D. The skill of production workers is enhanced by investments in Production Training. The motivation of the production workforce is built through investments in Profit-Sharing. The premise is that the more highly trained the production labor force and the higher their motivation, the more efficient they will be in producing your product and the less raw material will be required.

Process R&D is decision of Production Management but Production Training and Profit-Sharing are decisions of Human Resource Management. As long as you use a functional approach in the organization of your company, your functional specialist should recommend decisions in his/her area of responsibility. *The final decision, however, is a responsibility of the whole management team.*

Again, both of these effects reflect the growth curve and lagged-response.

If Sales Salaries and Profit Sharing (percent of after-tax profit that goes into the profit-sharing plan)are lower than the average for the industry, salespersons may voluntarily leave your company. In BUSPOG this effect is somewhat random-- they may or may not quit.

A similar situation exists for the Production Labor Force. When the Production Wage Rate and/or Profit Sharing is lower than the industry average, voluntary terminations from the production labor force may result.

The management of some companies may pursue a Human Resources Policy that minimizes the number of voluntary terminations. The management of other companies may adopt a policy to maintain a low level of wages, salaries and other benefits and adjust for voluntary terminations by recruiting more production workers and sales trainees than are actually needed. Perhaps the cost of continually hiring additional employees will be less than the cost of maintaining competitive wages and salaries. This decision depends upon the competitive environment and the judgment of management.

Human Resources Planning Procedure

The BUSPOG decision variables for the Human Resources Function have a pronounced effect on the demand for a company's products and on the Cost of Production. All five of these variables represent cost entries in the company's Income Statement and Flow of Funds Statement. If the values for these variables are not selected with care, poor profit and cash positions for the company may result. The procedure suggested in this section should prove helpful.

Human Resources Plan

The Human Resources Plan Form developed for the game (Table 9-1) facilitates the hiring and firing decisions affecting the Sales Force and the Production Labor Force. The top three sections of the form pertain to the Sales Force for each of the Three Markets; the bottom section pertains to the Production Labor Force. The Human Resources Vice-President obtains the desired sizes for the Sales Force from the Vice-President of Marketing and the desired size for the Production Labor Force from the Production Vice-President. The Human Resources Vice-President then estimates

Table 9-1

Human Resources Plan Form

(figures expressed in numbers of persons)

			Year 2				Year 3	Year 4
			Qtr 1	Qtr 2	Qtr 3	Qtr 4		
1	Market 1	Sales Force						
2		Sales Trainees						
3		Voluntary Terminations						
4		Adjusted Size						
5		Desired Size						
6		Required Change						
7	Market 2	Sales Force						
8		Sales Trainees						
9		Voluntary Terminations						
10		Adjusted Size						
11		Desired Size						
12		Required Change						
13	Market 3	Sales Force						
14		Sales Trainees						
15		Voluntary Terminations						
16		Adjusted Size						
17		Desired Size						
18		Required Change						
19	Production	Production Force						
20		Voluntary Terminations						
21		Adjusted Size						
22		Desired Size						
23		Required Change						

the anticipated voluntary terminations from each group and calculates the size and direction of change for each Sales Force and for the Production Labor Force.

Lines 1, 7, and 13 of the form are used to enter the size of the current Sales Force for each of the Three Markets. The values for these are found in the Production and Sales section of the Output Report for the past quarter.

The number of salespersons hired last quarter (and ready to begin selling this quarter) is listed in the Production and Sales section of the Output Report under Sales Trainees. These values should be entered on **Lines 2, 8, and 14** of Table 9-1. (Since newly hired salespersons spend the first three months of their employment being trained, Salespersons hired in one quarter do not begin selling until the following quarter. During the three months of their training they are paid regular Sales Salaries and participate in the company's Profit-Sharing.) The training these new employees receive is not the same as that facilitated by the Sales Training decision variable.

The decision variable on Sales Training, which sets the level for Sales Training Expenditures, is the amount to be spent for training all of the Active Sales Force. It is an expenditure to upgrade the professional selling skills of the Sales Force and is designed to enhance their effectiveness in selling activity. The training associated with orientation for new salespersons is included with the other costs of hiring new Sales Trainees.

Lines 3, 9, and 15 are for the Human Resources Vice-President's estimates of the number of Voluntary Terminations expected in each market. Since the number of voluntary terminations is somewhat controlled by two of the decision variables within the Human Resources Function, it seems appropriate that the Human Resources Vice President should be responsible for estimating this effect. The adjusted sizes on **Lines 4, 10, and 16** are found by adding the number of Sales Trainees to the size of the Current Sales Force and then subtracting the number of anticipated Voluntary Terminations.

The Desired Sizes of the Sales Force on **Lines 5, 11, and 17** are obtained from the Marketing Vice-President. The Adjusted Sizes are then subtracted from the Desired Sizes to obtain the Required Changes given on **Lines 6, 12, and 18.** These values are returned to the Marketing Vice-President for approval. Positive values indicate a need to hire Sales Trainees; negative values indicate a need to fire Active Salespersons.

The transfer of salespersons from one sales district to another is not allowed in BUSPOG. If a company wishes to expand its salesforce in one market and reduce it in another, it will have to hire in one and fire in another. As in the real world, each time an employee is hired or discharged, costs are incurred.

Unlike the situation for the sales force, production workers begin producing in the quarter in which they are hired; there are no trainees involved. The size of the current production Labor Force at the end of the last quarter of play is entered on **Line 19**.

Line 20 of the Human Resources Plan is used to enter the Human Resources Vice-President's estimate of the number of voluntary terminations in the Production Workforce. These projected estimates of Terminations should be based both on calculations and on subjective judgments. The Adjusted Size (**Line 21**) is found by subtracting the value for Voluntary Terminations (Line 20) from the value for Production Force (Line 19).

The Desired Size of the Production Workforce is obtained from the Production Vice-President and entered on **Line 22**.

The Required Change in the number of production workers to be hired or discharged is found by subtracting the value for Adjusted Size (Line 21) from the value for Desired Size (Line 22). This result is entered as the Required Change on **Line 23** and reported to the Production Vice-President.

Table 9-2

Wage and Salary Plan Form

		Year 2			Year 3	Year 4
	Qtr 1	Qtr 2	Qtr 3	Qtr 4	Total	Total
1 Sales Salary (In dollars/month)	1250	1250	1250	1500	1500	1700
2 Sales Training (in thousands of dollars)	15	15	20	25	120	160
3 Production Wage Rate (in dollars/hour)	5.25	5.25	5.25	5.50	5.50	5.75
4 Production Training (in thousands of dollars)	8	12	12	15	650	700
5 Profit Sharing (percentage)	0.3	0.3	0.3	.03	0.4	0.4

Wage and Salary Plan

The Wage and Salary Plan has the values for the Five Human Resources Decision Variables which are based on the policies of Human Resources. Table 9-2 shows an example. **Line 1** indicates this company intends to increase the quarterly Sales Salary in Year 2. The company also contemplates increasing the Sales Training budget to $25,000/quarter as shown on **Line 2**. The values on **Line 3** show that the company's Production Wage Rate will be raised from $5.25 to $5.50 per hour during year 2. The expenditure for Production Training is proposed to be increased to $15,000 (**Line 4**), and the after-tax profit of the company, which is to be distributed to the employees, is to remain constant at 0.3 percent (**Line 5**).

Summary

The procedure for the quarterly decisions of Human Resources management includes these steps:

1. From the Production and Sales section of the Output Report, find the size of the Current Sales Force, the number of Sales Trainees, and the size of the Production Labor Force. Enter these values on the Human Resources Plan.
2. Estimate the number of anticipated Voluntary Terminations in the Sales Forces of each of the Three Markets and in the Production Labor Force and enter these values on the Human Resources Plan.
3. Compute the Adjusted Sizes for the Sales Forces and the Production Labor Force.
4. Obtain the Desired Size of the Sales Force for each market from Marketing Management.
5. Determine the Required Changes in the Sales Forces and report these to Marketing Management.
6. Obtain the Desired Size of the Production

Labor Force from Production Management.

7. Determine the Required Change in the Production Labor Force and report this to Production Management.

8. Select values for the Sales Salaries expenditures for Sales Training, Production Wage Rate, expenditures for Production Training, and for employees' Profit-Sharing percentages.

9. Forward all Human Resource Decisions to Financial Management and the President.

As with the vice-presidents of the previous two functions the Human Resources Vice-President is required to interact and coordinate with all the other functional vice-presidents and the President.

Finance and Accounting Management

10

As indicated in the Overall Organizational Operations in Figure 2-1, the management of the Financial Function is concerned with both the sources and uses of funds for the company. The primary device used in the game for planning this aspect is the Three-Year Cash Budget that is updated at least once each quarter. The Cash Position of the company is a result of not only the five Financial Decisions but also decisions made in the other functional areas of Marketing, Production, and Human Resources.

The Financial Decisions for the company include:
1. Bonds Sold or Redeemed
2. Bank Loan Requested
3. Dividends Paid
4. Stock Issued
5. Savings Account Deposit or Withdrawal

In addition, the Financial Vice-President is responsible for the section of the Output Financial Reporting which includes an Income Statement, a Flow of Funds Statement, and a Financial Position Statement.

Effects of Financial Variables

Successful Financial Management for a BUSPOG company as well as for a real-world organization requires close coordination with Top Management, Marketing Management, Production Management, and Human Resources Management. Cash must be available to: meet the expenses resulting from the decisions in each of the management areas, make the interest and principal payments on Bank Loans, meet the expense of the company's bond program, pay dividends to the stockholders, and pay income taxes. *In the game, the company's ability or inability to properly manage its Cash has the primary effect on its credit rating.* When a company does not have sufficient cash to meet its obligations, the game automatically provides the company with the needed amount through a three-month Emergency Bank Loan.

An Emergency Bank Loan is different from a requested Bank Loan made through the second Financial Decision. The lending institutions assume there is more risk in making loans to an organization with unskilled financial management. When a company needs an Emergency Bank Loan because it has run out of cash, it signals that the organization has unskilled financial management. A requested loan has no effect on the confidence the creditors have in a company's management. Receiving an Emergency Bank Loan causes the interest rate for all bonds and requested loans to go up significantly. In effect, the company's credit rating is lowered, and its interest rates are raised. The result is -- the expense associated with all debt capital immediately becomes greater.

Since a company's Cash Position is so very important, the Financial Vice-President should find ways to control it through the Financial Decisions: **increase** the Cash Available through a Requested Short-Term (three month) Bank Loan, through a

Table 10-1
Cash Budget Form/Flow of Funds Statement

		Year ___				Year ___	Year ___
		Qtr.1	Qtr.2	Qtr.3	Qtr.4	Total	Total
1	Accounts to be received						
2	Bank Loans						
3	Bond Sale Return						
4	Savings-- Interest and Withdrawal						
5	Plant and Equipment Sale						
6	Stock Sale Return						
7	Beginning Cash						
8	Total Sources						
9	Production Costs						
10	Marketing Costs						
11	Other Costs						
12	Dividends						
13	Loan Repayment						
14	Bonds Redeemed						
15	Income Taxes						
16	Profit sharing Cost						
17	Plant & Equipment Investment						
18	Savings Deposit						
19	Total Allocations						
20	Ending Cash Balance						

Sale of Bonds or Stocks, or through a Savings Account Withdrawal. In addition, the vice president can **reduce** such expenditures as: the amount of funds used to pay dividends, redeem bonds, and make deposits if the savings account. The use of funds for the repayment of loans is not under the control of the Financial Vice-President. Since all loans are ninety-day notes, the principal and interest on Outstanding Bank Loans are paid automatically each quarter.

Besides affecting a company's Cash Position, the - decision to pay Dividends has another effect on the company's financial well-being. Specifically, the After-tax Income for a company can either be distributed to stockholders through Dividends or kept within the company as Retained Earnings. The more income that is distributed as Dividends, the higher the price of the company's stock. If a company anticipates Selling Stock to raise needed funds, it should consider the Effect of the Dividends on Stock Price.

A final effect of the Financial Variables is the Income from the Interest paid a company on its Savings Account Balance. The Savings Account option in the game provides a company with an opportunity to generate earnings from Cash that is not otherwise needed in the company's operations.

Financial Planning Procedure

The Financial Plan brings together all the projected results of a BUSPOG company. In particular, the forecasted financial outcomes are responsive to: the economic and competitive aspects of the business environment; the goals, strategies, and policies set by Top Management; the Marketing Plan and Sales Forecast from Marketing Management; the Production and the Raw Material Plans of Production Management; and the Human - Resources Plan and the Wage and Salary Plan developed by Human Resources Management. The Financial Plan unites all these elements into a Projected Cash Position, Income Level, and Financial Position.

Cash Budget/Flow of Funds Statement

The Cash Budget Form is provided to assist the Financial Vice-President in projecting a company's Cash Position. The categories in it are the same as those reported in the Flow of Funds Statement, thesecond financial statement Section 6 of the Output Report. The vice-president can compare expected results to those that actually are achieved. This comparison assists the vice president in assessing the methods of projecting the sources and allocations of funds.

An example of this form is given as Table 10-1. The top eight lines treat the Sources of Funds; the next eleven lines, the Allocations of Funds; and the last line, the projected Ending Cash Balance.

On **Line 1** enter the total funds to be collected during the quarter. All sales of a BUSPOG company are made on credit with an average collection period of one month. There are no bad debts. Accordingly, sales from the first month of a quarter are collected the second month of the quarter. Sales from the second month of a quarter are collected the third month of the quarter. Sales from the third month of a quarter are collected the first month of the next quarter. Thus two-thirds of the cash revenue in a quarter is collected in that quarter, and the other one-third is carried into the next quarter as Accounts Receivable. The amount entered on Line 1 of the Cash Budget is equal to two-thirds of the projected Sales Revenue for the current quarter plus the Accounts Receivable from the past quarter as reported in the Financial Position Statement, Section 4 of the Output Report.

When the Top Management Team agrees, the Financial Vice-President may request and obtain a short-term (one-quarter) Bank Loan. This is one of the Financial Management Decisions and is entered on **Line 2** on the Cash Budget form.

Another source of funds is the Sale of Bonds, which is entered on **Line 3**. In BUSPOG bonds are more like long-term variable interest loans than like bonds in the real world. The interest rate for bonds in the game is variable. If a company improves its Credit Rating, the Bond Interest Rate on both its Outstanding Bonds and Newly-Issued Bonds is reduced. Conversely, if a company's Credit Rating is lowered, the Bond Interest Rate increases.

Neither those bonds outstanding at the beginning of the game nor those issued during the game mature during the competition. However, any part of a company's Outstanding Bonds can be called at any time. When called, they are *redeemed at face value* plus a 6 percent *call premium*.

Line 4 of the Cash Budget allows an entry for withdrawals from a company's Savings Account plus interest paid on the past quarter's balance. Unless noted differently by the game administrator, the Interest Rate on a Savings Account is 8 percent per year throughout the game. The interest is paid to the company every quarter as opposed to being deposited in the company's Savings Account.

When the Top Management Team decides to reduce the Production Laborforce, the part of Plant and Equipment assets used by the former employees is sold. **Line 5** of the Cash Budget Form provides a place for listing the estimated funds from this source. There is both a fixed and a variable cost associated with this transaction; the variable cost is a function of the number fired.

The expected return from the Sale of a company's Common Stock is entered on **Line 6**. The total return equals the Number of Shares Issued times the Issue Price. The Issue Price equals (the Closing Price of the company's stock last quarter in Section 5 of the Output Report) times (the number of Shares Outstanding at the end of last quarter) divided by (the number of Shares Outstanding at the end of last quarter) plus (the number of Shares being Issued at this time).

The Cash available at the beginning of the quarter is entered on **Line 7**, and the sum of Lines 1 through 7 is entered for Total Sources on **Line 8.**

Lines 9, 10, and 11 are for entering the estimates for a company's Production Costs, Marketing Costs, and Other Costs. The Cost Estimates Form (Table 10-2) is provided to assist in determining these estimates. The suggested estimating procedure for the form will be discussed later.

The amount of Dividends to be distributed to the stockholders is the third Financial Decision. This value is entered on **Line 12**.

Line 13 presents the principal due on all outstanding Loans at the close of the last quarter. Remember all bank loans are 90-day notes and come due the quarter after they are made. For convenience, they are repaid automatically. If this is not a convenient time to repay them (if you do not have enough surplus cash) ask for another Bank Loan.

The amount of Bonds to be Redeemed, (the first Financial Decision), is entered on **Line 14.**

Estimated Income Taxes are entered on **Line 15.** The tax rate is 50 percent of Net Profit Before Taxes and is paid each quarter. The easiest way to estimate income taxes is to complete the Income Statement (Table 10-3) which is discussed later in this chapter. Until that statement is available, adjust last quarter's Income Tax to reflect anticipated changes in Sales and Costs.

Line 16 adjusts for the estimated cost of the company's Profit-Sharing Plan. This entry is calculated by subtracting Estimated Income Tax from Before Tax Profits and multiplying what is left by the percentage of profit sharing (the fifth Human Resource Decision). Remember the accountant's adage — always overestimate costs and underestimate income.

The estimate of the Cost of Plant and Equipment Investment appears on **Line 17**. When the Production Labor Force is increased, an investment in Plant and Equipment must be made in order that employees will have a place to work and equipment to use. This investment has both a fixed and a variable component; the variable component is a function of the number of employees hired.

Line 18 contains the amount of funds to be deposited into a company's Savings Account during the quarter.

Line 19 is a sum of all the Allocations in Lines 9 through 18. The value for **Line 20** is found by subtracting the value in Line 19 from the value in Line 8. If this calculation results in a negative Ending Cash Balance, the company needs to increase its sources of funds or reduce its disbursements. Failure to do this will result in a an Emergency Bank Loan for the company.

Cost Estimates

As promised earlier, you can obtain the cost estimates for Lines 9, 10, and 11 of Table 10-1 through the use of a form such as that shown in Table 10-2. The entries in this form duplicate those given in the Output Report (Section 3, Costs) except in two respects: First, the Production Cost given in the Output Report includes an entry for Depreciation, the Production Cost Section in Table 10-2 does not; second, the Cost of Raw Material in the Output Report is the value of the Raw Material actually used in production, while that in Table 10-2 is for the funds to be expended in the quarter to purchase Raw Material. The Cost Estimates of the Output Report are from the standpoint of Income; those of Table 10-2 are from the standpoint of Cash Flow.

If the Scheduled Production Work Week is forty or fewer hours, the Labor cost of **Line 1** in Table 10-2 is simply equal to (the Production Wage Rate)

times (40) times (the number of weeks in the quarter -- 13), times (the number of employees in the Production Workforce). If the Scheduled Work Week is greater than forty hours, all time over forty hours is paid at one and one-half times the wage rate.

The entry for **Line 2**, the Cost of Raw Material is equal to (the amount of Raw Material to be ordered this quarter) times (the Per-Unit Cost of Raw Material Ordered). The Per-Unit Cost of Raw Material Ordered is given in Economy and Stock Market, Section 5) of the Output Report for the prior quarter. In other words, the Per-Unit Raw Material Cost given on the *previous* output results always applies to the upcoming decision.

The Maintenance Cost of **Line 3** is a percentage of the Labor Cost: as productivity output per hour increases, the maintenance cost decreases and vice versa. This method for computing Maintenance Cost means that maintenance for overtime operation is also at one-and-one-half times the regular wage rate.

The Production Training Cost of **Line 4** is equal to the fourth Human Resources Decision.

The decision to either increase or decrease the Production Labor Force results in one-time Human Resources Costs which are entered on **Line 5**. When the labor force is increased, there are variable and fixed costs associated with hiring and training new employees. Conversely, when the labor force is reduced, there are fixed and variable costs associated with severing an employee's association with the company. To calculate these fixed and variable costs, such as costs of Production Level Change, refer to the discussion in Chapter 12 on Simultaneous Equations.

The Equipment Replacement Cost, **Line 6**, is a percentage of the Cost of Raw Material Used (based on a first in, first out evaluation -- FIFO). As the amount of raw material required per unit of finished product is reduced, the Equipment

Table 10-2

Cost Estimates Form

		Year ___				Year ___	Year ___
		Qtr. 1	Qtr. 2	Qtr. 3	Qtr. 4	Total	Total
	Production						
1	Labor						
2	Raw Material						
3	Maintenance						
4	Training						
5	Production Level Change						
6	Equipment Replacement						
7	Production Administration						
8	Total Production Cost						
	Marketing						
9	Advertising						
10	Sales Salaries						
11	Sales Commission						
12	Transportation						
13	Sales Training						
14	Sales Force Change						
15	Marketing Administration						
16	Total Marketing Cost						
	Other						
17	Research & Development						
18	Fin. Prod. Carrying Cost						
19	Raw Mat Carrying Cost						
20	Bond Interest						
21	Bond Call Premium						
22	Loan Interest						
23	Other Administration						
24	Total Other Cost						

Replacement Cost is reduced, and vice versa. Unlike Maintenance Cost, there is not a 50% increase in Equipment Replacement Cost for overtime operation.

The Production Administration cost of **Line 7** has a fixed component and a variable component. The latter is a function of the Total Production Output.

The sum of the seven production cost elements is entered on **Line 8** of Table 10-2 and on Line 9 of Table 10-1.

Line 9 of Table 10-2 begins the computation of the cost of Marketing. This entry is equal to the Advertising Expenditures for all Three Markets. The next item, Sales Salaries expense, is for the Active Salespersons plus the Sales Trainees to be hired during the current quarter. The value to be entered on **Line 10** is (the number in this Salesforce) times the (Monthly Salary for the quarter) times (three -- the number of months in the quarter).

The Sales Commission expense of **Line 11** is found by multiplying the Sales Commission percentage (the fifth Marketing Decision) times the estimated Gross Sales Revenue.

The Transportation charges for moving Finished Products to each of the three markets are:

Market	Transportation Charge
1	$ 8 per unit
2	$ 11 per unit
3	$ 5 per unit

The entry for **Line 12** is the sum of the number of units moved to each market times the respective charges for each of the three markets.

While the entry for Sales Training, **Line 13**, is equal to the value selected by Marketing Management, it is actually the second Human Resources Decision.

The entry for Sales Force Change, **Line 14**, is determined in a manner similar to that for Production Level Change, Line 5.

The final marketing expense, the cost of Marketing Administration, has one variable component that is a function of the total number of Active Salespersons and Sales Trainees, another variable component that is a function of the Total Number of Units Sold, and a fixed component. (Again, refer to the discussion of Simultaneous Equations in Chapter 12.) An estimate of this value is entered on **Line 15**. The Total of the seven Marketing Cost elements is entered on **Line 16.**

The Research and Development cost entered on **Line 17** is equal to the expenditures for both Product and Process Research and Development. Product Research and Development is the fourth Marketing Decision and Process Research and Development is the fourth Production Decision.

The estimated Carrying Cost for Finished Product Inventory **Line 18** is based on the Inventory Level at the beginning of the quarter. This carrying charge is primarily for warehouse storage and handling and to a lesser degree for inventory investment. Each of a company's three warehouses has an upper limit on storage capacity. If a company's Ending Finished Goods Inventory exceeds this capacity, the excess is stored in rented warehouses at a charge of $15 per unit per quarter as opposed to $4 per unit per quarter for storage in the warehouses owned by the company. The warehouse capacities are:

Market	Warehouse Capacity
1	150,000 units
2	150,000 units
3	100,000 units

The Carrying Cost for Raw Material Inventory is also based on the level of inventory at the beginning of the quarter. If this value is less than the warehouse capacity of 100 million pounds, the charge is $4 per 1,000 pounds per quarter. For material stored in excess of 100 million pounds, the charge is $15 per 1,000 pounds. The Estimated total for Raw Material Carrying Charge is entered on **Line 19**.

The quarterly expense for Bond Interest (**Line 20**) is equal to one-fourth of the Bond Interest Rate for a company (as specified in the Output Report for the last quarter) times the amount of Bonds Outstanding at the beginning of the current quarter. As previously mentioned, the Interest Rate on all bonds is variable within BUSPOG, with the value determined by a company's *credit rating*.

A company's bonds are callable with a Call Premium of 6 percent. The entry for **Line 21** is equal to 6 percent of the amount of Bonds to Be Redeemed during the quarter. The first Financial Decision indicates whether any bonds are going to be called.

The expense for Loan Interest of **Line 22** is equal to one-fourth the Interest Rate for a company as reported at the end of the previous quarter times the amount of the Outstanding Loans.

The expense for Other Administration is the Administrative Expense for the Human Resources function, the Financial/Accounting function, and the Top Management function. The first of these variable expenses is based on the number of employees, the second variable expense is based on the total gross sales, and the last expense is a fixed cost. (Again, refer to the discussion of solving simultaneous equations presented in Chapter 12.) The estimate for this administrative expense is entered on **Line 23**. The total of the seven Other Cost Elements is shown on **Line 24**.

Income Statement

For a company to remain in a competitive position in relation to its competitors, a *profit* must be produced. This does not mean that successful companies will realize a profit every quarter. Often, heavy expenses must be incurred in one time period in order that greater profits may be

generated in the future. If, however, a profit (that can be distributed to stockholders in the form of dividends, allocated to employees in the form of a profit-sharing plan, or returned to the company for financing future expenditures) is not produced over a longer time period, the company will not fare well in the competition.

To help ensure good profit-performance over a longer period of time, some approach to profit planning must be utilized. One such approach is to construct an Estimated Three-Year Income Statement. The form in Table 10-3 is designed to assist in this process.

On **Line 1** of this form the Estimated Gross Sales Revenue (as given on Line 19 of the Marketing Plan Form) is entered. On **Line 2** the value of the Finished Product Inventory at the beginning of the quarter is entered. The latter value is the same as the value of the Finished Product Inventory at the end of the last quarter as reported in the Financial Position Statement.

The Total Production Cost of **Line 3** is equal to the Total Production Cost calculated for the Cash Budget with two modifications. The first, is the value of Line 3 should include a charge for Plant Depreciation; the production cost for the Cash Budget does not include such a charge. Depreciation for each quarter is equal to 1 percent of the current value of the plant and equipment. The Plant and Equipment Value is given in the Financial Position Statement for the prior quarter. To make this first modification, one percent of the current Plant and Equipment Value is added to the Cash Budget Production Cost (Line 8 on Table 10-2).

The second modification to the Total Production Cost in the Cash Budget is an adjustment for the

Table 10-3

Income Statement Form

		Year ___				Year ___	Year ___
		Qtr. 1	Qtr. 2	Qtr. 3	Qtr. 4	Total	Total
1	Gross Sales Revenue						
2	Beginning Inventory						
3	Total Production Cost						
4	Goods Available						
5	Ending Inventory						
6	Cost of Goods Sold						
7	Gross Profit						
8	Marketing Cost						
9	Profit on Sales						
10	Other Costs						
11	Other Income						
12	Net Profit Before Taxes						
13	Income Taxes						
14	Net Profit After Taxes						
15	Profit-Sharing Cost						
16	Net Income						
17	Dividends						
18	Retained Earnings						

Cost of Raw Materials. The Raw Material cost for the Cash Budget computation is for the raw material purchased in the current quarter. The Raw Material Cost for the Income Statement is for the *raw material actually used for production* during the quarter. To make this adjustment, the Cost of Raw Material Ordered (Line 2 on Table 10-2) is subtracted and the value of the Raw Material Actually Used for production is added.

In summary, the modifications to the production cost are:

Production Cost for Income Statement =
    Production Cost for Cash Budget
    + Depreciation
    - Raw Material Ordered
    + Raw Material Used

The value for the Raw Material Used is computed in two steps. First, the value of the Raw Material Inventory given in last quarter's Financial Position Statement is divided by the Raw Material Inventory (Section 2, Production and Sales, last quarter's Output Report). This first step yields the average cost per pound for the available raw material . Second, this average cost per pound is multiplied by the Raw Material Required for this quarter's production (Line 3 of the Raw Material Plan).

The value of Goods Available for **Line 4** is found by adding the Total Production Cost of Line 3 to the Beginning Inventory value of Line 2.

The value of the Ending (Finished Product) Inventory is calculated separately for each of the three warehouses, then the sum of these three values is entered on **Line 5** of Table 10-3.

Before continuing, it should be recognized that there are two possible values for units in the Ending (Finished Product) Inventory. One value is for the units that were made this quarter (the cost of units produced this quarter) and a second FIFO

(first-in first-out) value for units that were made in previous quarters. The value of currently produced units is Total Production Cost for this quarter (Line 8 of Table 10-2) divided by Total Production Required (Line 13 of Table 8-1). The value of units produced in previous quarters is the value of the Finished Product Inventory (Line 3 of last quarter's Financial Position Statement) divided by the total number of units in the Finished Product Inventory reported in last quarter's Production and Sales section of the Output Report.

The calculation for each warehouse can be made in one of two ways.

In each market, if the number of finished products remaining in the forecasted Ending Finished Product Inventory (Desired Ending Inventory in Table 8-1) is less than or equal to the allocation to this market (Production Required in Table 8-1), then all of the units remaining in the inventory should be valued using the *current cost per unit*. If the forecasted ending Finished Product Inventory is more than the allocation to this market, the new units allocated to this market will be valued at the current cost per unit and the difference between Allocation and forecasted Ending Finished Product Inventory will be valued at the *FIFO cost per unit*.

The following example may make this explanation clearer. (Please refer to the information presented in Figure 10-1.)

For Market 1, the Desired Ending Inventory is less than or equal to units allocated; this means only currently-produced units make up the Ending Inventory, and they are valued using the current cost per unit. Accordingly, the value of the ending inventory equals the Ending Inventory times the current cost per unit.

In Market 2, the Desired Ending Inventory is greater than the number of new units allocated to this market; this means the excess units were produced in previous quarters. The second form of computation must be used. Since a FIFO inventory policy has been adopted, all of the units allocated to this market this quarter remain in the inventory, the difference between Allocation and Ending Inventory was manufactured in previous quarters. The value of the Ending Inventory is equal to the (number allocated) times (the current price per unit) plus (the difference between the number allocated and the ending inventory) times (the FIFO value).

In Market 3, the Desired Ending Inventory is again less than the Allocation; therefore, value of the Ending Inventory is the number of units remaining times the current price.

Figure 10-1
Calculation of Ending Inventory Value

| Total Production Cost | $30,028,000 |
| Total Production (units) | 144,375 |

From last quarter's data:

| Inventory - Finished Products | $27,968,000 |
| Finished Product Inventory | 149,487 |

	Market 1	Market 2	Market 3
Allocation	62081	53419	28875
Ending Inv.	56008	63318	1907

Total Production Cost	$30,028,000
Total Units Produced (units)	144,375
Current Cost /Unit	$207.99

From last quarter's data:

Inventory - Finished Products	$27,968,000
Finished Product Inventory (last qtr.)	149,487
FIFO cost/unit	$187.09

Market 1

Ending Inventory (units) < Allocation (units)

Ending Inventory ($) = (Ending Inventory $_{units}$)
    X (Current Cost/Unit)
    = (56,008)($207.99) = $11,649,103.92

Market 2

Ending Inventory > Allocation

Ending Inventory $ =
    (Allocation $_{units}$) X (Current Cost/Unit)
    + (Ending Inventory-Allocation)
        X (FIFO cost/Unit)
    =(53,419)X($207.99)
        +((63,318-53,419)) X ($187.09))
    =(53,419)X($207.99)+(9,900)($187.09)
    =$11,110,617.81+$1,852,191
    = $ 12,962,808.81

Market 3

Ending Inventory < Allocation

Ending Value = (Ending Inventory $_{units}$)(Current Cost/Unit)
    = (1907)($207.99) = $396,636.93

Ending Inventory=Market 1+Market 2+Market 3
Ending Inventory = $11,649,103.92 +
$12,962,808.81 + $396,636.93
    = $25,008,341.67

The Cost of Goods Sold on **Line 6** of Table 10-3 is equal to Goods Available minus the Ending Inventory value. The Gross Profit of **Line 7** is equal to the Gross Sales Revenue minus the Cost of Goods Sold. The Marketing Costs entered on Line 10 of Table 10-1 and Line 16 of Table 10-2 is placed on **Line 8** of Table 10-3 and subtracted from Gross Profit to yield the Profit on Sales for **Line 9**.

The Total of Other Costs from Line 11 of Table 10-1 or Line 24 of Table 10-2 is placed on **Line 10** of Table 10-3. The value for **Line 11** of Table 10-3 is the *sum of the income from two sources*. The first source is the quarterly interest paid to the firm on its Savings Account Balance. It is equal to the Savings Account Balance at the end of last quarter times 8 percent and divided by four. (Eight percent is the annual rate of interest on the savings account; this cost is for one quarter.)

The second source is the income from the Sale of Plant and Equipment as entered on Line 5 of the Cash Budget (Table 10-1).

To yield the value for Net Profit Before Taxes (**Line 12**) subtract Line 10 from the sum of Line 9 and Line 11.

Since the Income Taxes Rate is 50%, enter fifty percent of Net Profit Before Taxes on **Line 13** for the quarterly income tax payment.

To arrive at Net Profit After Taxes (**Line 14**) subtract Income Taxes (Line 13) from Net Profit Before Taxes (Line 12).

The quarterly employee Profit-Sharing Cost of **Line 15** is equal to the Net Profit After Taxes (Line 14) times the current profit-sharing percentage (the fifth Human Resources Decision). When the value of Line 15 is subtracted from Line 14, the result is the value of Net Income on **Line 16**.

Net Income can be paid to stockholders as Dividends (**Line 17**) or left within the company as Retained Earnings (**Line 18**).

Financial Position Statement

Whereas a Cash Budget provides a plan of the sources and uses of funds over the next accounting period and an Income Statement provides a calculation of profits over the same period, the Financial Position Statement provides an estimate of the financial condition of a company for the end of the next accounting period. In effect forecasting the values of these three financial statements builds what is usually called the Pro-Forma form of the Financial Statements. These are especially important to the stockholders and creditors of a company because they provide a means for judging the financial condition of the company. Maintenance of a favorable financial condition is assisted by estimating a company's financial position at future points in time. The form in Table 10-4 facilitates such a projection.

The top section of this form presemts the company's Assets and the bottom section, the company's Liabilities at the end of the time period.

The Current Assets include five items. The first, the Ending Cash Balance (**Line 1**), can be found on Line 20 of the Cash Budget (Table 10-1). The value for Accounts Receivable (**Line 2**) is equal to the Gross Sales Revenue value of Line 1 of the Income Statement (Table 10-3) divided by three, since the average collection period is one month.

The value of the Finished Product Inventory is taken from Line 5 of the Income Statement (Table 10-3) and entered on **Line 3** of Table 10-4.

The value of the Raw Material Inventory (**Line 4**) is equal to the value of the Raw Material Inventory from last quarter's Financial Position Statement minus the value of the Raw Material Used in production this quarter plus the value of the Raw Material Ordered this quarter.

The value of the Raw Material Used this quarter was computed when determining the cost of materials in the Production Cost for the Income Statement (Line 3 of Table 10-3). As described before, Raw Material Used is equal to the value of the Raw Material Inventory from the Position Statement last quarter divided by the number of pounds in the Raw Material Inventory reported in Section 2 of last quarter's Output Report multiplied by the Raw Material Required for production.

The Raw Material Ordered this quarter was calculated and is available as the Raw Material Cost used when estimating production costs for the Cash Budget. As such, it is available on Line 2 of

Table 10-4

Financial Position Statement

		Year ___				Year ___	Year ___
		Qtr. 1	Qtr. 2	Qtr. 3	Qtr. 4	Total	Total
1	Cash Balance	Total sounce − Total allocation					
2	Accounts Receivable						
3	Finished Product Inventory						
4	Raw Material Inventory						
5	Savings Account Balance						
6	Total Current Assets						
7	Plant & Equipment Value						
8	Total Assets						
9	Bank Loan Balance						
10	Bonds Outstanding						
11	Capital Stock Value						
12	Accumulated Retained Earnings						
13	Total Stockholder's Equity						
14	Total Liabilities						

the Cost Estimates Form (Table 10-2).

The final current asset noted on Ttable 10-4 is the company's Savings Account Balance at the end of the quarter which is entered on **Line 5**. The Savings Account Balance is the balance at the end of the last quarter minus withdrawals plus deposits. Savings Account transactions are the fifth

Financial Decision.

The Total Current Assets are the sum of Lines 1 through 5 and are entered on **Line 6**.

The only fixed asset in BUSPOG is the value of the company's Plant and Equipment. This value, which is entered on **Line 7** of the Position Statement, is equal to the Plant and Equipment

Value last quarter minus the plant Depreciation charge (previously estimated for the Production Cost in the Income Statement) plus or minus any change in plant and equipment resulting from a change in production capacity (the values of these changes were previously estimated for Lines 5 and 17 of the Cash Budget, Table 10-1.

The total of the current and fixed assets is entered on **Line 8** of the Position Statement.

Bank Loans are the only *current liability* in the game. The value of Bank Loans (both requested and emergency Bank Loans) is entered on (**Line 9**).

Bonds are the only *long-term liability*. This value is calculated by starting with the value noted in last quarter's Financial Position Statement minus the value of Bonds Redeemed this quarter plus the value of the Bond Sale Return (both values are available in the Cash Budget for this quarter). The current level of Bonds Outstanding is entered on (**Line 10**).

The projected Retained Earnings for the current quarter, (on the last line of the Income Statement, Table 10-3 are added to the Accumulated Retained Earnings from the Position Statement in the Output Report for the last quarter to arrive at the new value for Accumulated Retained Earnings (**Line 12**).

The Capital Stock Value on (**Line 11**) is equal to the Total Assets minus the Accumulated Retained Earnings, minus Bonds Outstanding and minus Bank Loan Balance.

Total Stockholders' Equity (**Line 13**) is equal to the sum of Capital Stock Value (Line 11) plus Accumulated Retained Earnings (Line 12).

The Total Liabilities (**Line 14**) equal the sum of Lines 9 through 13.

Summary

The procedure for Financial/Accounting Management Decision Making includes these steps:

1. Make estimates of all Production Costs, Marketing Costs, and Other Costs. These values can be entered on the Cost Estimates Form and then on the Cash Budget Form.

2. Based on data from the Output Report for the past quarter and the decisions of the other three vice-presidents, determine the values for the remaining Cash Budget entries.

3. Based on a sound Financial Plan, make the Five Financial Decisions and enter their values in the Cash Budget. Computation of values for the Cash Budget can then be made.

4. Using the same data complete an Income Statement. The primary difference between the Income Statement and the Cash Budget is in the computation of the Production Cost.

5. Complete the entries for the Financial Position Statement.

6. Forward all changes in Financial Decisions to the president.

7. Forward the results of the Cash Budget, Income Statement, and Position Statement to the president and the three other functional vice-presidents.

The completion of the Three Financial Statements may result in the conclusion that some of the decisions of the other three management areas may not be in the best interests of the company. The Top Management Team may have to redesign its strategies and/or policies and/or the decisions on Marketing, Production, and Human Resources. This process of *looping* from the decisions of the other management areas to the results of the projected in the financial statements and back again to the decisions could continue for some time.

As the team becomes more experienced, however, in performing its responsibilities in the economic and competitive environment of BUSPOG and, especially, in developing integrated spreasheets, this decision-making process will become more streamlined.

Using a Spreadsheet

11

From the beginning of personal or micro-computers spreadsheets have been about the most powerful application available . Now the power and sophistication of major spreadsheet programs like Microsoft's® Excel© bring most people about as close as they will get to writing their own programs. Using spreadsheet programs to support decision making in BUSPOG has proved to be quite useful -- almost as useful as learning how all of the areas in business fit together.

Why are spreadsheets so useful? Because once a spreadsheet has been built, complex calculations and extensive operations can be performed quickly and repeatedly with no further effort.

Spreadsheets have a number of uses in BUSPOG. For example, if you want to use quantitative and seasonal indexes when forecasting Demand, built-in quantitative formulas can routinely calculate weighted averages, trends, and seasonal indexes. They can also forecast the effect of various management decisions, such as changes in Price or level of advertising. They can even adjust for the lagged response in Marketing and Production variables.

 Another useful tool when forecasting Demand is graphing historical and other information. A visual examination of a line graph is easy, and short-range extrapolation is obvious.

Finally, a simple spreadsheet which calculates the percentage of error between different forecasts not only helps you select the most

accurate way to forecast but also helps you manage your Ending Inventories of Raw Material, Finished Product, and Cash.

Once you have an acceptable Forecast of Demand, spreadsheets can help make Production, Human Resource, and Financial decisions because the BUSPOG formulas are provided line by line. For example, if you establish a policy of maintaining an Ending Inventory which is a function of the size of the error between your Forecast of Demand and the Actual Demand) plus a factor which is (a function of the relative payoff when you make a Sale versus the Cost of not making a Sale), your spreadsheet can calculate Total Production, the number of Production Workers which will be required, and the Allocation of this Total Production to the Three Markets. Now that's support for your decision-making?

Spreadsheets can also be used to interpret your results. For example, if you divide Ending Finished Product Inventory in each market by the Demand in that market and multiply by 100, you get the Percentage of Demand that remains in the Ending Inventory. Comparing these market-to-market percentages gives an indication of the balance among your ending inventories.

If enough time is spent integrating your spreadsheet , ultimately you will come out with a simulation of the BUSPOG algorithm. If you have no error in your Forecast of Demand, you will know before the game is run (within rounding errors and the variation which occurs because of the occasional use of random numbers) what your results will be. In effect, you create pro-forma Financial Statements. Change your decisions, and you change your results. Should you use overtime or hire or fire employees to balance your production. What will be the payoff from the investments required to build Productivity? What will happen if you don't make these investments? In management theory, these are called "what-if" decisions. What will happen if I do this? or if I do that instead? Without an adequate simulation of reality, "what-if" decisions are based on pure speculation.

Skills Required in Spreadsheeting

The basic skills required for spreadsheeting are to know:
- what a sheet is
- how to move around inside a sheet
- how to create a range or block of information
- how to use filling
- how to copy formulas
- how to use Help
- how to create graphs

It is assumed that these skills have been gained by taking basic spreadsheeting classes or by completing the tutorial which is provided in most programs.

Experience shows, however, that in BUSPOG there are a number of skills required to complete even a minimum spreadsheet which are not known by most students. Some of these additional techniques will be reviewed.

In these discussions references will be made in relation to using Excel© Version 5.0 or higher, but there is always more than one way to use a spreadsheet. The process described here has been chosen because experience has shown it works and is easily understood by students with a minimum understanding of spreadsheeting.

Sheets vs. Books of Sheets

Older spreadsheet programs open new sheets which are treated as individual documents. Newer versions of the spreadsheet programs develop books which contain individual sheets. While you can use these older programs, in BUSPOG books are much easier to use.

The computer disk which accompanies this manual has individual sheets for each of the BUSPOG planning forms. If you are using a version of a spreadsheet program which does not make books of sheets, open the sheet or sheets that you want to work with. Remember that the **Window** button on the **Toolbar** will show you all of the documents that are open. Since each sheet is a separate document, you can move between sheets by clicking **Window** and then clicking on whichever open sheet you want at the moment.

If you are using a newer version of a spreadsheet program which forms books of related sheets, **copy each of the sheets** (on the disk accompanying this manual) into the **book** and **rename each sheet** for quick identification. To rename a sheet in Excel©, **click on Format>Sheet>Rename** and follow the prompts.

Linking Cells

It is extremely simple and fast to link cells in Excel©. **Start with the cell where you want the contents of another cell to appear**. (If you click the left mouse button while pointing to that cell, a heavier line will appear around the cell indicating it is the active cell.) Say to yourself "I want this cell to = this other cell." As you say this, **hit the "=" button on the keyboard and then click on the spreadsheet where the desired information exists, then click on the cell where it is. To end the link, press "Enter"** and you will return to the cell where you started and the desired information will be there.

Entering Formulas

Early in the game players begin to understand that both simple and complex formulas can be entered in any cell reducing the time spent in calculations. Unfortunately they frequently waste a great deal of time typing in cell addresses. Cell addresses can be entered very quickly by the linking process described above, and formulas can be built by entering the appropriate mathematical symbol between two linked cells. When the formula is complete, press "Enter". For example, on the **Production Plan Form**, Production Required (Line 4)=Sales Forecast (Line 1) plus Desired Ending Inventory (Line 2) minus Beginning Inventory (Line 3). To enter this formula when you are making decisions make Line 4 of the appropriate column your active cell. Say to your self "I want this cell to equal (**Press =**) this cell (**click on Line 1 of that column**) plus this cell (**push + from either the number pad or the keyboard and then click on Line 2**) minus this cell (**press - and click on Line 3**), then end the entry (**press "Enter"**). Excel will return you to Line 4 where you started. Whenever you enter a new formula, check the calculation on a calculator or use the results of an Output Report. Especially when the formulas are complex, be sure to group your calculations appropriately using parentheses to insure the proper order of calculation. Checking your answers is the only way to insure the accuracy of your formula

Copying Cell Contents

Cell contents, including links and formulas, can be copied from one cell to another in several different ways. Once the formula is performing correctly, copy it across all the columns you are using. The same calculation will be made each time you use the sheet.

If you set up a spreadsheet where all the calculations and links for one BUSPOG form are put in one column, that column will be copied across the next quarter and subsequent quarters and will also be correct (except data you enter into particular cells).

Suppose you have built a spreadsheet for your Production Plan where all the calculations for Year 3, Quarter 1 are done in Column C.

If you want the same formula to appear in every column. When you enter your data all calculations will be completed automatically. Now,
1. **Click on a cell which has a formula (C4)**
2. **Create a range of cells from C4 to the right edge of your sheet**
3. **Click Edit>Fill>Right**

Conditional Branching Programs

Conditional Branching Programs (sometime called "If" statements) considerably enhance the power of most spreadsheets. The idea is to test to see whether or not a particular situation is true. If it is, you will do one thing. If it is not, you will do something else.

Like most activities on spreadsheets, there are several ways to develop "If" statements. The simplest way is to type the statement.

Suppose you want to enter a series of data in Column A ranging from Row 1 to Row 20. You want to know how many of these data points are above ten. In Row C categorize each entry according to whether it is above ten by using an "If" statement. Then sum the number of times an entry is above 10.that they are.
1. Make the cell where you want the test to be made your active cell. **Click cell (C1)**
2. **Type = if (**
3. Select data to be tested **Click cell A1**
4. Define the test **Type >10**
5. What to do if the test is true, **Type ,1**
6. What to do if the test is false, **Type ,0**
7. Close the parenthesis, **Type)**
8. Close the equation, **Press Enter**

The final equation in your active cell C1 will be: =if(A1>10,1,0) What this equation says is that if the data in A1 is more than 10, put a 1 in this cell, otherwise put a 0.

Copy this equation down Column C. When data is entered in Column A, a "1" will appear in Column C when the data is over "10" and a "0" will appear when the data is under "10". If we sum Column C in C21, we will know how many datapoints exceed "10".

The test (A1>10) is very simple in this example but it can be as complex as the situation requires. What to do if the test is true(Step 5) and What to do if the test is false (Step 6)can also be as complex as the situation requires.

When you need to make more than one test before a result is calculated, you will need to use "Nested If" statements. For example, when you calculate the cost of hiring or firing Production Employees (Production Level Change). There is a fixed and a variable cost when you fire people, a different fixed and variable cost when you hire them, but if you don't hire anyone, there is no cost. The problem is that if you make a single test (if Labor Force Change is less than "0"), you fired Production Workers and you use the constants for firing. If that test is not true, you might have hired people or you might have done nothing (Labor Force Change = 0). If you use the constants for hiring, the variable term will go to "0", but the fixed charge will remain.

In this case you would first test to see if the Labor Force Change =0. If so the charge =0. If this is not true, it must be either more or less than "0" so you do a new "If" statement on the "what to do if false" entry (For example, test to see if Labor Force Change is less than "0".) If that statement is true, calculate Production Level Change using the fixed and variable costs for firing. If it is false, use the fixed and variable costs for hiring. While this is a simple calculation, the prose description may seem confusing, ask the game administrator to explain the procedure.

92

Spreadsheets Vary in Complexity

In BUSPOG there are two different levels of complexity at which spreadsheets may be built. At one end of the continuum is what might be termed a minimum spreadsheet. At the other end is a completely integrated spreadsheet. Effective spreadsheets can vary from one end of the continuum to the other.

Minimum Spreadsheet

The computer disk which comes with the player's manual already has pro-forma spreadsheets in an Excel© format for each of the planning forms described in Chapters Seven to Ten. These forms have been modified to have a column for each of the quarters for a year of play. Additional years can be copied and pasted to fit the length of your game. Freezing the frame at the beginning of Quarter One allows you to slide the columns containing data under the columns containing descriptions of the contents. Each form is a spreadsheet.

In addition, the Pro-Forma Production Plan and the Pro-Forma Raw Material Order Form have the calculating formulas already installed which allows you to begin using these sheets anytime. The sooner the formulas for the other sheets are put in place, the sooner you will obtain adequate support for your decision-making (and the sooner you can abandon *SWAGS*).

In a minimum spreadsheet you can make as many assumptions and shortcuts as you choose as long as they have a rational base. You can also insert as much data as many times as you want. The spreadsheet, in this case, is primarily summing various entries and performing simple arithmetic.

At the minimum, you need a Marketing Plan, Production Plan, Raw Materials Plan, Human Resources Plan, and a Cash Budget.

To make a minimum spreadsheet will probably

take between five and ten hours; it depends on your skill.

Integrated Spreadsheet

At the other end of the continuum of spreadsheet-complexity is what might be termed an Integrated Spreadsheet.

Data in an Integrated Spreadsheet is entered only once in a special new data section. Data from the previous quarter's Output Report can be imported directly.

The various sheets are linked to allow the needed data to be picked up automatically from the New Data Section. Decisions that are calculated (e.g., Labor Force Change or Allocations) are linked directly to the appropriate place in the Decision Sheet for the current quarter. Those that are not calculated (e.g., Price or Investment in Process R&D) are linked directly from the New Data Input Sheet to the Decision Sheet.

In all ten planning forms formulas are in place and accurate. When necessary, "if--then" statements are used to calculate accurately regardless of the decision (e.g., Labor Costs will be correct whether or not you use overtime).

Again, depending on your skill to complete an integrated spreadsheet will probably take between 25 and 40 hours of work.

Building The Minimum Spreadsheet

A minimum spreadsheet, which can be built in five hours, is recommended in order that you can experience the value of a spreadsheet managing a BUSPOG company. Depending on the desires of your game administrator, the sophistication of the sheet can be increased (and accompanied by a commensurate increase in grade and/or honor) until you have a fully integrated sheet which simulates the BUSPOG model.

Six of the ten planning forms presented in this manual can form the backbone of a minimum spreadsheet:

- Marketing Plan Form
- Production Plan Form
- Raw Material Plan Form
- Human Resources Plan Form
- Cash Budget Form
- Cost Estimates Form

In a minimum spreadsheet, you can type as many numbers into cells as you find necessary, make as many estimates, and take as many shortcuts as you choose as long as you can justify what you have done. For example, the Cost of Hiring a person can be estimated by dividing the cost of Production Level Change in an output report by the Number of People Hired. Even greater accuracy can be achieved later as you learn more sophisticated and more accurate ways to calculate this cost. Similarly, Income Taxes for this quarter can be estimated as a little more than last quarter because of an estimated small rise in Gross Sales Revenue.

The simplest calculations, such as the summing of several entries or a simple multiplication or division, can also be accomplished. As more sophistication is added and more linking occurs, the grade or honor can be increased.

To aid in the building of a minimum spreadsheet, the ten planning forms used in BUSPOG are supplied on the computer disk which accompanies the player's manual. In addition, the formulas to calculate Total Production Required, Production Force Required. Allocation to each market, and Raw Material to Order are already on the Production Plan Form and the Raw Material Plan Form.

Building The Integrated Spreadsheet

In an integrated spreadsheet two new sheets are created: a Decision Sheet, which collects decisions to be entered into BUSPOG, and a Data Input Sheet, which contains all information needed. In addition to the six planning forms required for the minimum sheet, the integrated spreadsheet requires the Income Statement and the Financial Position Statement . 93

In an integrated spreadsheet, as stated previously, all information is entered only once (on the New Data Input Sheet). The different planning forms obtain the data needed through direct links. All constants are calculated. All contingencies are controlled by "If" statements (e.g., methods are determined to calculate straight time as well as overtime pay; an "If" statement determines which case prevails). All decisions are linked to their sources.

To test the accuracy of an integrated spreadsheet enter the data from an Output Report (demand, sales, price, etc.) and check for differences between the results calculated on the Spreadsheet and the results in the Output Report.

For an experienced spreadsheet builder an integrated spreadsheet may require fifteen to twenty hours of work beyond a minimum spreadsheet, but it should receive a grade commensurate with such an investment in time.

Enhancements

Regardless of the level of sophistication of the spreadsheet a BUSPOG team may build, there is an almost unlimited number of small spreadsheets which teams can create to make decision-making easier and more accurate. While these enhancements are in no way as difficult to build as an integrated spreadsheet, the creativity and personal involvement they require should be amply rewarded with extra credit, or a boosting in overall spreadsheet grades.

Enhancements are not too difficult to build and provide information to support and/or enrich decision-making. The simplest enhancements merely supply proportions, ratios, or percentages. For example, working from information in Section Six of the Output Report you can evaluate the effectiveness of your Production Workers compared to those of your competitors (within the limits imposed by the accuracy of the data in this section) by dividing Production Output by Production Work Force to get Production per Worker. Divide Unit Sales by Sales Force to get Sales per Salesperson for each team. Is your Sales Force competitive? Sum Unit Sales for all the companies to get Total Sales for the industry. Divide your Unit Sales by Total Sales to get Market Share for both you and your competitors. With a little thought you can find all kinds of enhancements to support your decision-making.

Finally, you can integrate information from your Output Report with information about the whole industry which your game administrator may share with you. When you have accurately determined the Levels of Inventories and Financial Reserves of all your competitors and tracked changes through information in Section 6 of your Output Report, you will know almost everything about each competitor. This knowledge will help you discern their strategies and then counter with more effective strategies.

Quantitative Techniques

12

The Business Strategy and Policy Game provides an excellent opportunity to practice using all of the knowledge and skills that have been acquired in grade school, highschool, and undergraduate classes.

Almost from the beginning of the educational experience, students start to build their knowledge of the theory and skill and in applying numerical and mathematical techniques. Unfortunately, unless it is used, much of this knowledge is quickly forgotten (once credit for the course is gained).

The Business Strategy and Policy Game helps to recover much of this learning because using it improves the results achieved by a Buspog company. A few examples follow.

Ratios

Ratios, simply relating one number to another, is the simplest of the procedures through which a number representing one entity (e.g., the number of units in a Finished Product Inventory) is related to a number representing another entity (e.g., Demand in the previous quarter). In some cases, ratios are useful because the numbers stay the same and are easy to identify. A major problem with using pure ratios is that the ratios themselves are frequently difficult to equate to other ratios because the numbers which make up the ratios are different.

For example, in Year 2, Quarter 4 in Market 1 you have 56008 units in the Finished Product Inventory; Demand for the same quarter is 72822. In Market 2, you have 63318 units in the Finished

Product Inventory, and Demand is 61900. In Market 3, you have 1907 units in the Finished Product Inventory, and Demand for Market 3 is 37907.

Market 1	Market 2	Market 3
56008	63318	1907
72822	61900	37907

Identify the magnitude of the problem posed by the balance among your ending inventories from these three ratios. These pure ratios are difficult to equate.

Percentages

Percentages are only one step more complex than ratios but are much more useful and are used much more.

In most school systems students learn how to calculate percentages in the third grade, but it is amazing how many college students have forgotten how to calculate simple percentages.

To review: you calculate what percent a number "A" is of a second number "B" by dividing "A" by "B" and then multiplying by 100. (Actually, if you are willing to work with proportions rather than a percentages, you don't have to multiply by 100.)

The procedure can be applied to the example presented in the discussion of ratios to achieve a more meaningful mathematical relationship.

	Mkt 1	Mkt 2	Mkt. 3
End. Inv.	56008	63318	1907
Demand	72822	61900	37907
	77%	102%	5%

If you have an inventory policy that Ending Finished Product Inventories should be 30% of Demand, you can see that Markets 1, and 2 are considerably overstocked while Market 3 has almost stocked out. This makes it clear that the present pattern of allocation needs to be questioned (the percentages should be about 30%) and perhaps the level of production as well. (Markets 1 and 2 have too much inventory.)

Percentages are also useful in deciding amounts to be invested in Process or Product Research and Development. In these cases you might compare the percentage of Gross Sales invested in Process and Product Research with the percentage invested by real world companies in your industry.

Percentages are also useful in evaluating the relative effectiveness of your Sales Program. If Market Share is increasing, your Sales Program must be more effective than your competitors. If Market Share is decreasing, one or more competitors have a more effective program than yours.

Market Share is your percentage of the Total Market in your industry. Total Market (Total Sales) in your industry can be calculated by summing the Unit Sales of all the companies in Section 6 of the Output Report. Your Market Share is calculated by dividing your sales by total sales. You can also calculate the Market Share of your competitors in the same way. Plotting the Market Shares of all companies in your industry, quarter by quarter, will show which companies are gaining and which are losing Market Share. This, in turn, might lead to questioning the effectiveness of your marketing plan.

Arithmetical Calculations

Everyone understands how to do simple arithmetical calculations (addition, subtraction, multiplication, and division), yet it is amazing how few players use arithmetical skills compared to the large number who try to get by using subjective guesses (SWAGs) without any mathematical support for their decisions. The following are a few ways to use arithmetic to support BUSPOG decisions.

Current Cost Per Unit

Your company can survive in the *short-run* if you price your products to cover only Production Costs. In the *long-run,* however, products must be priced to cover Total Costs. Too often, BUSPOG managers price their products in relation to the prices of their competitors or some other criterion and then wonder why profits elude them.

In the real world companies do sell their products at a loss, but when they do occur, they have a reason for doing this (e.g., to increase Market Share or to attract customers who make other purchases which makes up for the loss on the one item). Management's plan how the company will recover from the experience. Certainly, real-world managers know the cost of their products.

Current Cost Per Unit is easily calculated using simple arithmetic. Simply divide Total Cost in dollars by Total Production in Units.

To summarize:

Current Cost Per Unit = Total Cost $_{Dollars}$ / Total Production $_{Units}$ And

Total Cost $_{dollars}$ = (Production Cost+Marketing Cost+Other Cost) X 1000 Thus,

Current Cost Per Unit=((Production Cost + Marketing Cost + Other Cost) X 1000) / Total Production in units.

Determining the Amount of Production

It becomes much easier to make Production and Human Resources decisions by using a formula which requires only simple arithmetic skills.

Total Production = (Number of Production Hours $_{quarter}$) X (Productivity) And

Number of Production Hours $_{quarter}$=(Production Workers) X (Production Scheduled $_{hours/week}$) X (13 $_{weeks/quarter}$). Therefore,

Total Production = (Production Workers) X (Production Scheduled $_{hours/week}$) X (13 $_{weeks/quarter}$) X (Productivity).

This is a powerful formula you can see to figure out:

1. The number of Units of Production you are going to get, knowing the size of your workforce, the number of hours you plan to work, and your productivity.
2. The number of Production Workers you need if you want a particular level of production. (Solve for Production Workers by moving all other factors from above to the other side of the equation)
3. The number of Production Hours you need to schedule if you want a particular level of Production. (Solve for Production Hours Scheduled $_{week}$ by moving all other factors to the other side of the equation).
4. The Balance between Production Workers and necessary Production Hours per week can also be calculated by using Equation No. 2 and various Production Hours. If you put the equation into a spreadsheet, the solution becomes even easier. When you change the variable inside the equation, the spreadsheet will change the variable which is outside. This is especially effective if you also build a formula which calculates Labor Cost. If you include an "If" statement to accommodate for overtime (if hours/week >40) and tease out the equation for Production Level Change (Line 5 of Table 10-2), you can determine whether it is

better to adjust the number in the labor force or use overtime. (This is exactly what you do when you build an integrated spreadsheet to calculate Production Costs.)
5. The payoff from increasing or reducing Productivity can be evaluated using the equation described in the preceding example. This time change is the number for Productivity first up then down, hold hours constant, and observe the change in the number of Production Workers.

Arithmetic/Algebra

One of the unique aspects of BUSPOG is the way it demonstrates the use of quantitative techniques without making them the center of attention. For example, it is not too difficult to build a complete pro-forma simulation of the game because all of the formulas for all of the calculation forms are given line by line in Chapters 7 through 10. While most of these formulas are simple and straightforward, some require figuring out constants for the formulas.

In some instances, an equation needs a *single constant* (e.g., Maintenance is a percentage of the Cost of Labor). Several equations have *two constants* (e.g., Production Administration has a *fixed* constant and a *variable* constant which is a function of Total Production). Marketing Administration and Other Administration require *three constants*. These particular formulas are ideal demonstrations of ways constants can be determined through the application of arithmetical and/or algebraic techniques to historical data.

Single constants are extremely easy to calculate. For example, to identify what percentage should be used when calculating the Cost of Maintenance (Line 3, Production Cost Section, Cost Estimates Form, Table 10-2), simply divide the Cost of Maintenance by the Cost of Labor from the appropriate Output Report.

Two unknown constants are a bit more difficult to calculate because they require the learner to use skills from ninth-grade algebra -- namely the solution of simultaneous equations. From the Players Manual we learn that:

The Production Administration cost of Line 7 in the Cost Estimates Forms Table 10-2 has a fixed component and a variable component; the latter is a function of the total production output.

The first step in calculating these two constants is to write this statement as a general formula:

Production Administration = Fixed Constant + ((Variable Constant) X (Total Production $_{Units}$))

Next go to two printouts (Output Reports) of the results of running the game (when you are solving for two constants you need to have two equations) and select the necessary figures. For examples select the data from the reports for Year 2, Quarters 4 and 3 in Appendix A.

First, the general equation:

Prod. Adm.= Fixed + ((Variable)(Total Production $_{Units}$))

A. $1122000 = $ Fixed + Variable (144375)
B. $1093000 = $ Fixed + Variable (138516)

Subtracting "B" from "A" we get:

C. $29000 = $ Variable (5859)
(The *Fixed Constants* terms cancel when you subtract one Fixed from one Fixed.)

To solve for the Variable constant:

Variable $= 29000/5859 = 4.9497$

Substitute this value for the Variable constant in either equation A or equation B

A. $1122000 = $ Fixed + Variable (144375)
$1122000 = $ Fixed + 4.9497 (144375)
$1122000 = $ Fixed + 714612.93

Now solve for the Fixed constant:

D. Fixed $= 1122000 - 714612.93$
Fixed $= 407387.1$

To check your calculations, substitute the Fixed and Variable values into your second equation:

B. $1093000 = $ Fixed + Variable (138516)
$1093000 = 407387.1 + 4.9497(138516)$
$1093000 = 407387.1 + 685612.64$
$1093000 = 1092999.7$
which rounds to 1093000

Solving a problem with three constants is more complex.

From the Players Manual we learn that:
"The final Marketing expense, Marketing Administration Cost, has a variable component that is a function of the Total number of active Salespersons and Sales Trainees, another variable component that is a function of the Total number of Units Sold, and a fixed component."

Again, the first step in identifying these three constants is to write this statement as a general formula:

Marketing Administration = Fixed + ((Variable 1) X (Active Salespeople + Trainees)) +((Variable 2) X (Total Sales $_{Units}$))

Use three printouts of the results of running the game (when you are solving for three constants you need to have three equations). Select the necessary figures. In this case, let us use the data in the Output Reports for Year 2, Quarters 4 and 3 and 1 from Appendix A.

Mkt. Adm. $= F + V_1$(Salesforce) $+V_2$(Units Sold)

A. $2963000 = F + V_1(60) + V_2 (172629)$
B. $2953000 = F + V_1(55) + V_2 (180640)$
C. $2652000 = F + V_1(48) + V_2 (134388)$

Now subtract B from A and C from A. Call these new equations X and Y. (In each case the *fixed constants* terms cancel.)

X. $10000 = V_1(5) + V_2(-8011)$
Y. $311000 = V_1(12) + V_2(38240)$

There are several ways to proceed but the easiest is to cross multiply the coefficients of V_1

X. $10000(12) = (V_1(5)(12) + V_2(-8011) X (12)$
Y. $311000(5) = (V_1(12)(5) + V_2(38240)) X (5)$

X. $120000 = V_1(60) + V_2(-93132)$
Y. $1555000 = V_1(60) + V_2(191200)$

To make the numbers easier, this time let's subtract "X" from "Y" to obtain a new formula "Z".

Z. $1435000 = V_2 (284332)$

And now solve for V_2

$V_2 = 1435000 / 284332 = 5.0469$

Substitute this value into equation Y:

Y. $311000 = V_1(12) + V_2 (38240)$
$311000 = V_1(12) + (5.0469) (38240)$
$311000 = V_1(12) + 192933.45$
$118066.55 = V_1(12)$
$V_1 = 118066.55 / 12 = 9838.8791$

And now substitute the values for V1 and V2 into equation A to obtain the *fixed constant*.

A. $2963000 = F + V_1(60) + V_2 (172629)$
$2963000 = F + (9838.8791) X (60) +$
$2963000 = F + 590332.74 + 871241.3$
$2963000 = F + 1461574$
$F = 2963000 - 1461574 = 1501426$

To check the solution, substitute the derived values for the three constants into equation C.

C. $2652000 = F + V_1(48) + V_2 (134388)$
$2652000 = 1501426 + ((9838.8791) X(48)) +$
$((5.0469) X (5.0469) X (172629)(134388))$
$2652000 = 1501426 + 472266.19 +$
678242.79
$2652000 = 2651934.9$ (rounds to 2652000)

Note: If you check these figures on a hand calculator, make sure you are working with at least eight digits to the left of the decimal point. Here too it is much easier to construct a spreadsheet

Forecasting Techniques

Forecasts are the way of life in BUSPOG. Every quarter you make forecasts of:
- Demand in each market
- Stockout Effect in each market
- Productivity
- Raw Material Requirements
- Asking Price for Raw Material
- Voluntary Terminations

and many others consciously and unconsciously.

There are many ways to forecast what is going to happen. Some are more accurate than others. Some require more time, energy, and knowledge than others. Generally speaking, the more accurate forecasting techniques require more time, energy, and knowledge.

Before discussing the standard approaches to forecasting, it should be pointed out that the only criterion to use when choosing a forecasting technique is the accuracy of the resulting forecast. Suppose you want a forecast of demand for your product in Market 1 next quarter. Several forecasting techniques, would provide several forecasts. You would choose the technique resulting in the forecast that is the closest to the actual Demand in Section 2 of your Output Report.

Guesses

The easiest and quickest way to forecast is to simply guess--and there is nothing wrong with guessing if you can guess accurately. Research has shown that some people can guess more accurately than others. Another way to forecast which takes a little more time and energy is to combine the guesses from a number of people; for example, you might poll the members of your group. Sometimes the multiple guesses are combined by averaging them. Sometimes accuracy is checked, and the guess of the most accurate forecaster is used.

Expert Opinion

Expert opinion is the most commonly used approach to forecasting. The Sales Forecast Form (Table 7-2) is an example of an *Expert Opinion* approach to forecasting.

There are both advantages and disadvantages to the *expert opinion* approach. The primary advantage of an approach like that presented in the Sales Forecast Form (Table 7-2) is it provides a quite complete list of the variables which may or may not influence the demand for your product.

The primary disadvantage is that, without further calculation, the assumed influence of each of the listed variables is in reality a guess. For example, you are asked to guess the effect on Demand of an increase or decrease in Price. At the beginning of play especially (when this form is most usually used), the effect of an increase or decrease in Price is pure conjecture. Then, to make matters absolutely impossible, you total these guesses to make a single adjustment to last quarter's Demand. Once the individual guesses are summed, there is no way to find out which of the guesses are accurate and which are actually counterproductive.

This is not to say that there is no advantage to using this approach. It is an excellent way to experience the frustration which comes from using a forecasting approach that provides bad forecasts, but it destroys the only way to discover which part is good and which part is not — which requires a great deal of data.

Primarily because of a lack of data, in BUSPOG there is no foolproof way to calculate the effect of the three economic variables (Gross Domestic Product, Personal Consumption Expenditures, and Household Formations) and the seven Marketing Variables (Price, Advertising, Sales Force Change, Product R&D, Sales Commission, Sales Training, and Profit Sharing); these values remain informed but subjective guesses.

Forecasts Based on Historical Data

A primary advantage of using the Sales Forecast Form is it focuses attention on the numerous variables which may have a significant influence on the changes in the level of Demand. For example, Backorders very definitely influence the level of Demand. Backorders are added directly to anticipated changes in Demand caused by the historical trend or seasonality. Trend can be estimated by either linear or multiple regression. Seasonality can be removed from historical data by dividing each data point by the appropriate seasonal index. Forecasts are then re-seasonalized by multiplying the forecasted value by the seasonal index.

Details on using these quantitative techniques are not discussed here because they are readily available in texts on the subject.

An alternative to basing forecasts on the effect of individual factors is using other quantitative techniques which pay no attention to the condition of individual variables. These techniques base their forecasts on the trends and tendencies of the total historical data.

Moving Averages

The most basic approach to forecasting a future event based solely on historical data is to assume that whatever the cause, the next event will be the same as the last event. This approach, usually called a *naive forecast*, has one redeeming feature

-- while it will not likely be the most accurate, it will probably be in the correct ball park.

The second most basic approach to forecasting the next event is to *average* all of the available data and divide by the number of data points. The next event is forecast to be the average of the previous data points. The advantage of this approach is it will minimize the effect of individual spontaneous deviations. A disadvantage is that it tends to smooth over the effect of consistent trends.

Moving averages is an approach that improves on both of these. When using a moving-average approach, an average is calculated for a limited set of data (e.g., the last four quarters), and this average becomes the forecast. Spontaneous deviations are smoothed and consistent trends are considered because the oldest quarter is dropped, and the newest is added as time progresses.

Weighted moving averages are a little more sophisticated; additional weight can be placed on the most recent or on some other data point to compensate for some other pertinent variable.

Details on using these approaches are readily available in standard textbooks on quantitative techniques.

Proportions

An approach to forecasting frequently used by BUSPOG players is calculating proportional increases. Here divide (the difference between the last two values by the last value) and add the resulting proportion of the last value to the last value. For example, it is quite simple to calculate the difference between Productivity indexes reported in the last two output reports and divide that difference by the last quarter's index. The result will be the proportional increase which should be added to last quarter's index to forecast Productivity for this quarter. (The same result is gained if you merely add the difference to the last value but it is generally easier to interpret the proportional changes.)

This is probably a good place to demonstrate how a forecast can be based on both objective data and on subjective judgment. Suppose you have determined that Productivity is changing about .37 each quarter, so that, if all things remain the same, you expect Productivity next quarter to be at .112. But not everything will be the same because you have just changed your investment in Production Training from $25,000 to $75,000 per quarter. Obviously, Productivity will be better than .112 but how much better is a subjective judgment.

This approach is less accurate when there is noticeable seasonality. It can be modified, however by calculating the percent increase from the same quarter of last year or by de-seasonalizing the data and re-seasonalizing the resulting forecast.

Exponential Smoothing

One of the most popular approaches BUSPOG players use to forecast demand is *exponential smoothing* The general formula presented in most textbooks on quantitative methods is:
Forecasted Demand for next period =
> Demand for this period + (the difference between last period and the period before)
> X (a smoothing coefficient)

Which smoothing coefficient to use depends on which gives the least error.

Discussions and illustrations are readily available in textbooks for quantitative techniques classes.

Linear Regression

A second method of forecasting Demand and perhaps most popular is the use of a technique called *linear regression* or *straight-line regression*.

Perhaps it will be easiest to summarize this approach to forecasting by asking you to imagine two intersecting lines. The horizontal line is labeled the X axis, and the vertical axis is the Y axis. The axes meet at their 0 points. Numbers on the X axis increase to the right and numbers on the Y axis increase as they go up.

The general formula for Linear Regression is:

Forecast for next period = Y + (T) (X)

Y = the Y intercept (the place where your regression line crosses the Y axis.

X = The slope of the line (the rise on the Y axis for every one unit on the X axis).

T = The time period for which you are making the forecast.

Discussions and illustrations are available in textbooks for quantitative techniques classes.

Other Quantitative Techniques

The level of this discussion, the large number of variables which the BUSPOG model simulates, and the limited amount of data generated in the normal playing period make it difficult to use many of the more sophisticated quantitative methods such as *multiple regression, non-linear regression, correlation, and multiple correlation.*

Incidentally, this is probably an appropriate time to mention that the f_x on the Excel® toolbar will lead you into formulas for all these and many other techniques. Excel® also has a well-developed **Help** section.

Graphing

Graphs are a unique and very efficient way to interpret data and make forecasts. It is very unusual to read an informative article in a newspaper or a periodical without having to interpret the content of a graph.

If you give almost any person a ruler, a piece of paper, and a set of colored pens, he/she can figure out a way to present data on some kind of a graph. Unfortunately, graphing takes time — unless you use a spreadsheet. Once you learn to use the Excel®Chart Wizard, you will never make another graph manually. All you need is your data, access to an Excel® program, and the ability to click that icon on the toolbar that looks like a barchart.

Try it, once you spend a few minutes exploring this function. you will be amazed how easily you can make very good-looking charts.

If you plot demand on the Y axis of a line graph and time period on the X axis, you will have an excellent picture of your growth in demand over time. Extend the line one or two periods (the process is called *extrapolation*), and you will have a very respectable forecast of Demand. Plot the demand of your competitors on the same line, graph, and you will see how your competitor's company is doing in relation to them.

Once players learn to graph on a spreadsheet program, it is amazing how many data series they find that need graphing.

Incidentally, graphing provides one way to evaluate the payoff from investments in those variables with a lag in effect. For example, plot investments in Advertising this quarter against Demand in succeeding quarters and see where the relationship is strongest.

Error in Forecasts

A prime reason teams can have problems in BUSPOG is they repeat ineffective decisions, based on either incorrect forecasts or on incorrect assumptions.

The best way to correct your assumptions is to study this manual closely, observe the effects of your decisions, and, as a last resort, ask the game administrator.

The best way to improve your results is to improve the data on which you are basing your decisions, and the best way to improve your data is to improve your forecasts -- by adjusting them to fit the outcomes. Of course, you cannot adjust your forecasts if you don't analyze how far off they are and in what direction.

There are at least three reasons why you need to know the size and direction of the error between forecasted value and actual value of the variable in question:

1. *To improve the quality of future forecasts.* (Adjust your next forecast by the direction and size of the error.)

2. *To compensate for anticipated errors.* Ending Inventories are in reality safety stocks which are maintained to compensate for a margin of error. The size of Ending Inventories the should partially be a function of the size of the error in related forecasts.

3. *To identify changes in the external environment.* Changes in the size and/or direction of the error between forecasted values and actual values are the first, and frequently the only, indication that something has changed in the external environment. When errors in a forecast change in a new but consistent way, the forecast and also the decisions based on the forecast must also change.

Every quantitative methods textbook available presents discussions about testing the accuracy of forccasts. Generally they suggest indices like *mean squared error* (MSE) or *mean average deviation* (MAD). Here is a simple arithmetical formula which is all you need to calculate the size and direction of the error in your forecasts:

Percent Error = (Actual outcome - Forecasted Outcome) / Actual outcome) X 100

It will take fewer than five minutes to build a spreadsheet to calculate the error in forecasts. If you link this sheet to your *output reports*, calculations will be made automatically. There is a great advantage to graphing the error in your forecasts each time they are calculated. An unexplained change in the size of your error is the best signal that something has changed in either the industry, the broad environment, the task environment or your internal situation.

Simulation

13

The end of the interaction with The Business Strategy and Policy Game seems an appropriate time to discuss the process of simulation and ways it might be used by real world organizations. While more and more data are becoming available, we also have more and more capability to do more and more complex manipulations of these data.

When interacting with BUSPOG you have interacted with a complex simulation of a manufacturing industry. At the heart of this simulation is a very large mathematical model (a series of simple and not so simple mathematical equations). These were designed and implemented in such a way that your decisions and the decisions of your competitors were converted into various output reports.

Simulation Defined

Simulation, in its most general form, is a procedure which describes a process by developing a model of that process. It then conducts a series of organized trial-and error experiments to predict the behavior of the process over time. To identify how the real world process would react to particular changes, you introduce these changes into the simulation and assume the reaction of the simulation approximates the reaction of the real process.

Many different kinds of models are routinely used in simulations. For example, scale models of airplanes (or parts of airplanes such as sections of the airplane's wing) are frequently built, and the behavior of the model is observed in a wind tunnel. When the competition for the America's Cup is in the news, we frequently read that a particular boat has a hull that was perfected by studying the effects of design changes on the performance of models in a testing pool. This too is simulation.

By far, the most usual model in simulations today is a mathematical model. Mathematicians have known for a long time how to build equations that duplicate any curve. As simulations get more and more complex, the models include highly complex equations to clocks, means, standard deviations, tables of random numbers to simulate probability, etc.

Simulation Accuracy

Models differ greatly in their ability to predict accurately the outcome of the process being simulated. While models predict the outcome of the process very accurately; other models are quite inaccurate.

Accuracy of a simulation depends on two variables: the complexity of the process being simulated and the complexity of the simulation model.

If the process being simulated is very simple and deterministic, there is no need for a complex model. For example, if every Finished Product requires 220 pounds of raw material, you can calculate the Raw Material Required next quarter by multiplying Production Required (in units) times 220. A simple dynamic requires only a simple simulation.

On the other hand, if the process being simulated is complex and probabilistic while the simulation model is simple and deterministic, then the simulation's results will not be very accurate.

If the purpose of the simulation does not require highly accurate results or if it is easier to compensate for the inaccuracy (by carrying safety stock, for example), then a simple simulation model or even a rule-of-thumb may be all that is needed.

The point to be remembered is that simulation models vary in their accuracy -- depending on the complexity of the process being simulated and the complexity of the simulation model. Any process, no matter how complex (even a flight to the moon) can be simulated to any level of accuracy given enough time, enough skill, and enough resources.

Uses of Simulations

Although some mathematicians insist that simulation should be used only when more accurate analytical approaches do not work, it turns out that simulation is one of the most widely- used quantitative techniques.

In a recent issue of Technology Review (September/October, 19989), Michael Dertouzos, questioning the wisdom of putting computers on every student's desk, said, "Certainly the promises of (using) computers for learning are impressive. Simulation, for example, is already a proven winner. Besides pilots, tank commanders in the Gulf War who spent a great deal of training time on tank simulators attest to the success of this approach. Simulation can be nicely extended to other kinetic and quantitative tasks such as learning how to drive, ski, swim, and sail, and, someday, even perform surgical operations. . . . The bolder notion of computer apprenticeship,

where a Frank Lloyd Wright simulator analyzes your architectural drawings as the great master might have done, is still in the imagination stage."

Examples of State-of-the Art Simulation

CACI in San Diego was one of the very early pioneers in providing software for building for simulations. Their original program was *Simscript*, their newest program is *Modsym*.

You can get an idea of current uses of simulation by visiting their website at **www.caciasl.com**. You will find the demonstrations and, after registering, you will be able to download free any of nine simulations:

- Parking Demo. Animated parking lot simulation (929k)
- An animated F-15 simulation (700k)
- A sonar emulation training tool (725k)
- Satellite Communication Demo. With scenario editor (956k)
- Sparing Logistics Demo. Prototype with scenario editor - a true Windows application (3,863k)
- Tank Battle Demo. An animated tank battlefield simulation (583k)
- Platform Demo. Satellite communication model (630k)
- Invader Demo. A space invader-type game (577k self-extracting zip file)
- Warfare Demo. A Gulf War demo (4,120k)

Simulation of BUSPOG

If you made a fully-integrated spreadsheet which predicted the outcome of your decisions within rounding error, you created a simulation like that of the BUSPOG game. Consider for a moment the value of having this simulation even if what you built was not perfect. Think how much easier the decisions became once you could use a Decision Support System (DSS); for example, as the basis for deciding how much Raw Material to order or how many Production Workers to hire.

You could evaluate the effectiveness of alternative decisions (like hiring more production workers or using overtime) by trying one decision and then the other decision but basing your final decision on the simulated outcomes. This is truly "what-if" decision-making. While you could always override the recommendations, these previously subjective decisions now have an objective foundation.

If you went on to develop some innovative enhancements to your spreadsheet, you had an objective basis for subjective judgments about, for example, the relative effectiveness of your Sales Force. You could determine if you were doing enough to enhance your sales activity. If you were tracking and perhaps plotting the size of the error between the Forecast of Demand and Actual Demand, you were the first to know when some factor in your sales environment had changed. If you were tracking the size of your competitors Ending Finished Product Inventories, you knew where they started, how many units they made, how many they sold, and the probable size of the error in the data. You also knew when to increase the size of your Ending Inventories in order to get all the extra sales possible.

In short, having a simulation of The Business Strategy and Policy Game made managing your company easier and a lot more effective.

Simulation in a Real-World Company

In Chapter 2, when introducing the basic concepts of the game, we pointed out that the BUSPOG computer program incorporates a number of hypothetical relationships. Some of these relationships relates the companies to the economic environment of the industry. Others relate the companies to each other. A third group of relationships relate the internal dynamics of each company. All of these relationships represent a conceptualization or model of how such an industry and its environment might behave. We also pointed out, although it was developed with a concern for realism, the model is actually a considerable simplification of the real world. You undoubtedly know by now, however,

how much the BUSPOG model simplified managing the complexity of the company.

Imagine for a moment that you are employed in a real company in a real industry with about the same responsibilities you had in the BUSPOG game. Only now you are faced with all the additional complexity which exists in the real world. Instead of having to manage the one item of Raw Material you have to manage eighty-seven different items of raw material (paint, pinch rollers, solenoids, etc.) and fifteen subassemblies which are purchased from outside suppliers. Since outside suppliers are people just like you they do not always deliver when they say they will; even when they do deliver on time, not all of the assemblies work as they are supposed to while the real problems are a lot more complex, but the dynamics are not that much different.

In BUSPOG we simulate a single variable Raw Material. In the real world we could simulate all the complexity of managing eighty-seven items of raw material and fifteen subassemblies. The model would be a great deal more complex, but it could be done.

The BUSPOG model assumes, when you invest in Research and Development, your returns will be in proportion to your investment until you reach an upper limit. This is seldom true in the real world. Sometimes you may get a lot of return for a little investment, but sometimes you may get no return at all. Can this complexity be simulated? Definitely! Would it be difficult? Not really. You merely gather data about your company's experience with R&D and build a model which reflects this experience.

The BUSPOG model also assumes that when you invest in Production or Sales Training, you always get a change in behavior and that change is always positive. This too is a simplification of reality since training programs aren't always effective. In fact, they can be counterproductive. Can this complexity be simulated? Yes, it can.

There are many other complexities in the real world. Not all Production Workers are the same. You always have more than one product. Credit is not always available. There are many kinds of advertising. Not all advertising costs the same. There are different kinds of advertising, some are more effective in different markets at different times in the product life-cycle. All these are true in the real world, and all of them can be simulated.

Every time you simulate increased complexity, you make it more difficult to understand what the simulation is all about--but it can be done. Is it worth doing is the question.

Imagine that you have built a simulation model of your real company which reflects all or most of the complexity of your Broad Environment, your Task Environment, and your Internal Situation. Suppose you and the other managers collectively understand and trust this model as completely as you now know and trust BUSPOG. Imagine how your management would change.

Recall how much more easily and effectively you could manage your BUSPOG company. When you built your spreadsheet. With a sufficiently complex simulation of your real company, wouldn't your management again become easier and more effective? Couldn't you determine which salespeople to keep and which to let go? Couldn't you decide which production workers need what kind of training and which service technicians should repair what kind of equipment?

Wouldn't an adequate simulation model in place change the process of setting, implementing, and controlling *operational goals?* Of course. It would also change *tactical and strategic planning.*

We seem to have entered an era in which more and more data about every aspect of our personal, professional, economic, and social lives is becoming available. At the same time the capability to utilize this data in more and more complex ways is also increasing. If you have a choice, what data do you want? What will you do with it?

One answer, especially when you are working with a system as large and as complex as an industrial organization (or a subsystem of an industrial organization), is to build a simulation of your system. When the results of the simulation are different from actual results in a statistically significant way, modify the dynamics of your simulation model. At the same time, modify your hypotheses about the cause-effect relationships in your system.

Conclusion
14

At the beginning of our discussion of The Business Strategy and Policy Game we assumed the game would be played by two kinds of learners: those just beginning to study the complex world of business and those playing the game as part of a capstone experience to bring the unconnected information of introductory courses in the various subdivisions of business into some kind of an integrated whole.

Those players just beginning to study the complex world of business usually leave this manual about the end of Chapter 5. This summary, therefore, is intended primarily for the advanced learners playing the game as part of a capstone experience.

The Business Strategy and Policy Game incorporates a conceptualization or model of how an industry and its environment might behave. Although the model was developed with a concern for realism, it is a considerable simplification of the real world. Because this has been stated previously, about specific areas of study, such as Finance or Production.

What does seem useful at this point is to bring together some of the **insights that players consistently report at the end of a BUSPOG experience**:

> The experience vividly demonstrates that what happens in one part of the company influences all the other parts, -- all parts of company activity are interconnected. Indeed they emphasize they learn to respect those areas of business about which they knew least and previously valued least. For example, Marketing

specialists learn most about Production or Information Systems; Information Systems People Learn most about Marketing.

No part of an organization is always the most important. Said another way, the most important part of an organization depends on what problems need to be solved. When Productivity is so low the company is losing money each time a sale is made, Production is the most important. When inaccurate and erratic Sales Forecasts create chaos, Forecasts of Demand are the most important. As the problems change. the relative importance of different functions changes.

Decisions need all the support they can get, spreadsheets are most often identified as providing the major insight gained in the BUSPOG experience. Students point to their new skills in building integrated spreadsheets. And how much easier and more effective decisions became once spreadsheets were completed. Almost all agree if they could repeat the experience, they would push harder to get the spreadsheet done sooner. While most players come to this experience knowing that a DSS is a Decision Support System it is not until they experience the support a well-constructed spreadsheet provides that they truly appreciate the value of objective calculations. Indeed it becomes rather difficult to make the point that, although decisions should be based on objective information, the ultimate choice must still combine objective data with intuition.

What you want to achieve determines what you do. While academic business programs are frequently criticized for teaching students to optimize Net Income in the short run rather than the long run, Net Income in the long run is not necessarily the factor to emphasize either. Once the BUSPOG experiences are combined with integrated *strategic, tactical* and *operational planning*, it becomes possible to demonstrate that quarterly results build toward achieving tactical goals and ultimately the *mission* and *vision*. Optimizing long-run Net Income is important only if this Net Income is part of achieving the mission and vision.

Decision-making is a group process not an individual process. At the beginning of a BUSPOG session, almost all BUSPOG teams organize themselves along functional lines: One person assumes responsibility for mastering the Marketing decisions, another becomes the expert on Production decisions, another takes responsibility for Finance and Accounting, etc. Such an arrangement works quite well if these functional experts get good results. Problems arise, however when the functional specialists begin to believe they have the right to make all of the decisions in their area of expertise, and their less than expert decisions are less than effective. Such a time provides an excellent opportunity to demonstrate that the results are what is important, not the protection of individual turf. Before the group meetings of management the functional specialists should prepare recommendations and then present them to the group; the management team may or may not adopt then. BUSPOG decisions should never be a series of discrete judgments by functional specialists.

Another insight players note is the importance of preparing for the unexpected. The possible but unexpected result always creates a challenge which some BUSPOG teams master but most do not. Teams tend to pick one number for their Forecast of Demand and plan in order to meet that number. The more successful BUSPOG teams consider the *range* of possible Demand and Sales and plan their operations across the range. They look to immediate past results and assess the likelihood that the past will be repeated. If Demand is at the top of the range and continues at that level for a quarter or two, how much Raw Material should be ordered? What if competitors continuously stockout? Preparing for the unexpected is a valuable edge to have in BUSPOG and the real world.

Finally players become aware of the importance of testing the *hypotheses*. All animals, including human beings seem to have an innate sense that there is a connection between what we do (our actions) and what happens around us. The action causes the result. If we know the cause-effect relations in a particular situation, we can control what happens -- by doing what causes that particular condition.

Anyone can make a hypothesis that there is a connection between a specific cause and a specific effect. People do it all the time. Some of these hypothesized cause-effect relations are true. Some of them are false. Some of them happen some of the time. Some of them hardly ever happen. Some of them used to be connected but aren't any more. Some of them were never connected before but are becoming connected now. The true cause-effect relationships are very hard to determine because they are always changing.

The only way **to identify which hypothesized**

cause-effect relationships actually help you control your environment is to describe objectively the effect you expect from an action. and then observe if it actually occurs. If it does, your hypothesis is strengthened. If it does not, your hypothesis is weakened. The only proof of your hypotheses is the capability to predict the effect.

Hypothesis-testing is the heart of the scientific method, it bloomed in the eighteenth century in what has come to be known as The Enlightenment. Many people, including most scientists, believe that the only way to identify which hypothesized cause-effect relationships are valid is to state the expected results and determine if they happen..

BUSPOG gives ample opportunities to test the hypothesized cause-effect relationships. For example, when you raised your price, did you make more profit? Was the cost of supporting more salespersons in Market 3 covered by a sufficiently large increase in overall sales?

Hypothesis-testing must be continuous. Only when the results are predicted ahead of time and the results evaluated, can the hypothesis be tested. Without *hypothesis-testing*, you lose the advantage of objective processes.

Appendix A
Historical Data

COMPANY 1   INDUSTRY 1   YEAR 1   QUARTER 1

1. DECISIONS

	MARKET 1	MARKET 2	MARKET 3
PRICE ($/UNIT)	250.	250.	225.
ADVERTISING ($1000/QTR.)	275.	275.	150.
SALES FORCE CHANGE (NO.)	2	2	2
PRODUCT R & D ($1000/QTR.)	37.		
SALES COMMISSION (%)	0.3		
PROFIT SHARING (%)	0.0		
SALES SALARIES ($/MONTH)	1000.		
SALES TRAINING ($1000/QTR.)	5.		
PRODUCTION TRAINING ($1000/QTR.)	2.		
PRODUCTION WAGES ($/HR.)	5.00		
PRODUCTION SCHEDULED (HOURS/WEEK)	40.		
LABOR FORCE CHANGE (NO.)	0		
ALLOCATION TO MARKETS (%)	35.	35.	30.
PROCESS R & D ($1000/QTR.)	37.		
RAW MATERIALS ORDERED (MILLION LBS.)	60.		
BONDS SOLD OR REDEEMED ($1000)	0.		
BANK LOAN REQUESTED ($1000)	3000.		
DIVIDENDS PAID ($1000)	0.		
STOCK ISSUED(1000 SHARES)	0.		
SAVINGS ACCOUNT ($1000)	0.		

2. PRODUCTION AND SALES

	MARKET 1	MARKET 2	MARKET 3	TOTAL
PRODUCTION WORKFORCE (NO.)	3000			
PRODUCTIVITY (UNITS/MAN-HOUR)	0.112			
RAW MATERIAL REQUIREMENTS (LBS./UNIT)	143.			
PRODUCTION OUTPUT (NO. OF UNITS)	61095	61095	52367	174557
FIN PROD INVENTORY (NO. UNITS)	49542	50982	43685	144209
RAW MAT INVENTORY (MILLION LBS.)	67.003			
DEMAND (NO. OF UNITS ORDERED)	36553	40113	28682	105348
SALES (NO. OF UNITS SOLD)	36553	40113	28682	105348
SALES ($1000)	9138.	10028.	6453.	25620.
SALESMEN ACTIVE (NO.)	13	13	5	31
SALES TRAINEES (NO.)	2	2	2	6

3. COSTS

PRODUCTION ($1000)

LABOR	7800.
MATERIAL	8749.
MAINTENANCE	1170.
TRAINING	2.
PROD LEVEL CHANGE	0.
EQUIPMENT	875.
ADMINISTRATIVE	1273.
DEPRECIATION	500.
TOTAL	20368.

MARKETING ($1000)

ADVERTISING	700.
SALARIES	111.
COMMISSIONS	77.
TRANSPORTATION	1423.
ADMINISTRATIVE	2397.
SALES FORCE CHANGE	50.
TRAINING	5.
TOTAL	4762.

OTHER ($1000)

R & D	74.
CARRYING-FIN PROD	300.
CARRYING-RAW MAT	128.
BOND INTEREST	750.
LOAN INTEREST	33.
ADMINISTRATIVE	3192.
BOND CALL PREMIUM	0.
TOTAL	4477.

4. FINANCIAL STATEMENTS

INCOME STATEMENT ($1000)

GROSS SALES REVENUE	25620.
BEGINNING INVENTORY	9750.
TOTAL PRODUCTION COST	20368.
GOODS AVAILABLE	30118.
ENDING INVENTORY	16827.
COST OF GOODS SOLD	13291.
GROSS PROFIT	12329.
TOTAL MARKETING COST	4762.
PROFIT ON SALES	7567.
TOTAL OTHER COST	4477.
TOTAL OTHER INCOME	20.
NET PROFIT BFOR TAXES	3110.
INCOME TAXES	1555.
PROFIT SHARING COST	0.
NET INCOME	1555.
DIVIDENDS PAID	0.
RETAINED EARNINGS	1555.

FLOW OF FUNDS STATEMENT ($1000)

ACCOUNTS COLLECTED	25620.
BANK LOANS REQUESTED	3000.
BOND SALE RETURN	0.
SAV ACCT-INT & WITHDRAWAL	20.
PLANT & EQUIP. SALE	0.
STOCK SALE RETURN	0.
BEGINNING CASH	11000.
TOTAL SOURCES	44100.
TOTAL PRODUCTION COST	32120.
TOTAL MARKETING COST	4762.
TOTAL OTHER COST	4477.
DIVIDENDS PAID	0.
LOAN REPAYMENT	1000.
BONDS REDEEMED	0.
INCOME TAXES	1555.
PROFIT SHARING COST	0.
PLANT & EQUIP. INVEST.	1555.
SAVINGS ACCT. DEPOSIT	0.
TOTAL DISBURSEMENTS	43913.
CASH AVAILABLE	187.
EMERGENCY BANK LOAN	0.
CASH BALANCE	187.

FINANCIAL POSITION STATEMENT ($1000)

CASH BALANCE	187.
ACCOUNTS RECEIVABLE	8540.
INVENTORY-FIN. PROD.	16827.
INVENTORY-RAW MAT.	23451.
SAVINGS ACCT BALANCE	1000.
TOTAL CURRENT ASSETS	50005.
PLANT & EQUIP. VALUE	49500.
TOTAL ASSETS	99505.
BANK LOAN BALANCE	3000.
BONDS OUTSTANDING	30000.
CAPITAL STOCK VALUE	63950.
ACCUM. RET. EARNINGS	2555.
TOTAL STOCK. EQUITY	66505.
TOTAL LIABILITIES	99505.

5. ECONOMY AND STOCK MARKET

GROSS NATIONAL PRODUCT 117. ($BILLIONS)   12. ($BILLIONS)
NUMBER OF HOUSEHOLD FORMATIONS 392. (1000.S)
PERSONAL CONSUMPTION EXP.--DURABLES
RAW MATERIAL COST 0.39 ($/LB.)

COMPANY	STOCK PRICE	EARNINGS	AVERAGE ADVERT.	SALES CUMM.	PROFIT SHARING	DIVIDENDS	SALES SALARIES	SHARES	PROD. WAGES	BOND INTEREST	LOAN INTEREST
LOSSES UNLIMITED, INC.	10.66	0.26	226.	0.31	0.0	0.0	1022.	6000.	5.13	10.0	13.0
UNAWESOME FOURSOME ASSN.	10.66	0.26	229.	0.30	0.0	0.0	974.	6000.	4.66	10.0	13.0
BOZO PRODUCTIONS	10.66	0.26	241.	0.29	0.0	0.0	986.	6000.	4.71	10.0	13.0
DIVERSIFIED, INC.	10.66	0.26	228.	0.31	0.0	0.0	996.	6000.	5.14	10.0	13.0
THE SYNDICATE	10.66	0.26	225.	0.31	0.0	0.0	958.	6000.	5.17	10.0	13.0
THE BENDDKEMPF CORP.	10.66	0.26	231.	0.31	0.0	0.0	1044.	6000.	5.00	10.0	13.0
UNETHICAL, INC.	10.66	0.26	238.	0.29	0.0	0.0	1015.	6000.	5.05	10.0	13.0

6. INDUSTRY ESTIMATES

COMPANY	AVERAGE PRICE	AVERAGE ADVERT.	SALES CUMM.	EARNINGS	PROD. WORKFORCE	PROD. OUTPUT	SALES FORCE	UNIT SALES
LOSSES UNLIMITED, INC.	235.	226.	0.31	0.26	3057	175235	30	105584
UNAWESOME FOURSOME ASSN.	252.	229.	0.30	0.26	3115	172806	32	104198
BOZO PRODUCTIONS	245.	241.	0.29	0.26	2833	175993	30	115264
DIVERSIFIED, INC.	235.	228.	0.31	0.26	3044	179079	33	105813
THE SYNDICATE	240.	225.	0.31	0.26	3042	171373	29	107431
THE BENDDKEMPF CORP.	241.	231.	0.31	0.26	2997	173218	32	102086
UNETHICAL, INC.	249.	238.	0.29	0.26	2864	167258	31	110229

COMPANY 1   INDUSTRY 1   YEAR 1   QUARTER 2

1. DECISIONS

	MARKET 1	MARKET 2	MARKET 3
PRICE ($/UNIT)	250.	275.	225.
ADVERTISING ($1000/QTR.)	300.	300.	175.
SALES FORCE CHANGE (NO.)	2	2	2
PRODUCT R & D ($1000/QTR.)	37.		
SALES COMMISSION (%)	0.3		
PROFIT SHARING (%)	0.0		
SALES SALARIES ($/MONTH)	1000.		
SALES TRAINING ($1000/QTR.)	4.		
PRODUCTION TRAINING ($1000/QTR.)	5.		
PRODUCTION WAGES ($/HR.)	5.00		
PRODUCTION SCHEDULED (HOURS/WEEK)	40.		
LABOR FORCE CHANGE (NO.)	10		
ALLOCATION TO MARKETS (%)	35.	35.	30.
PROCESS R & D ($1000/QTR.)	37.		
RAW MATERIALS ORDERED (MILLION LBS.)	0.		
BONDS SOLD OR REDEEMED ($1000)	0.		
BANK LOAN REQUESTED ($1000)	0.		
DIVIDENDS PAID ($1000)	0.		
STOCK ISSUED(1000 SHARES)	0.		
SAVINGS ACCOUNT ($1000)	0.		

2. PRODUCTION AND SALES

	MARKET 1	MARKET 2	MARKET 3	TOTAL
PRODUCTION WORKFORCE (NO.)	3010			
PRODUCTIVITY (UNITS/MAN-HOUR)	0.103			
RAW MATERIAL REQUIREMENTS (LBS./UNIT)	154.			
PRODUCTION OUTPUT (NO. OF UNITS)	56611	56611	48524	161746
FIN PROD INVENTORY (NO. UNITS)	55086	55160	56045	166291
RAW MAT INVENTORY (MILLION LBS.)	42.032			
DEMAND (NO. OF UNITS ORDERED)	51067	52433	36164	139664
SALES (NO. OF UNITS SOLD)	51067	52433	36164	139664
SALES ($1000)	12767.	14419.	8137.	35323.
SALESMEN ACTIVE (NO.)	15	15	7	37
SALES TRAINEES (NO.)	2	2	2	6

3. COSTS

PRODUCTION ($1000)		MARKETING ($1000)		OTHER ($1000)	
LABOR	7826.	ADVERTISING	775.	R & D	74.
MATERIAL	8740.	SALARIES	129.	CARRYING-FIN PROD	577.
MAINTENANCE	1174.	COMMISSIONS	106.	CARRYING-RAW MAT	268.
TRAINING	4.	TRANSPORTATION	1318.	BOND INTEREST	750.
PROD LEVEL CHANGE	11.	ADMINISTRATIVE	2628.	LOAN INTEREST	98.
EQUIPMENT	874.	SALES FORCE CHANGE	50.	ADMINISTRATIVE	3682.
ADMINISTRATIVE	1209.	TRAINING	5.	BOND CALL PREMIUM	0.
DEPRECIATION	495.				
TOTAL	5448.	TOTAL	5013.	TOTAL	5448.

4. FINANCIAL STATEMENTS

INCOME STATEMENT ($1000)		FLOW OF FUNDS STATEMENT ($1000)		FINANCIAL POSITION STATEMENT ($1000)	
GROSS SALES REVENUE	35323.	ACCOUNTS COLLECTED	32088.	CASH BALANCE	3434.
BEGINNING INVENTORY	16827.	BANK LOANS REQUESTED	0.	ACCOUNTS RECEIVABLE	11774.
TOTAL PRODUCTION COST	20332.	BOND SALE RETURN	0.	INVENTORY-FIN. PROD.	20836.
GOODS AVAILABLE	37160.	SAV ACCT-INT & WITHDRAWAL	20.	INVENTORY-RAW MAT.	14711.
ENDING INVENTORY	20836.	PLANT & EQUIP. SALE	0.	SAVINGS ACCT BALANCE	1000.
CUST OF GOODS SOLD	16324.	STOCK SALE RETURN	0.	TOTAL CURRENT ASSETS	51755.
GROSS PROFIT	18999.	BEGINNING CASH	187.		
		TOTAL SOURCES	32295.	PLANT & EQUIP. VALUE	49021.
TOTAL MARKETING COST	5012.			TCIAL ASSETS	100776.
PROFIT ON SALES	13987.	TOTAL PRODUCTION COST	11097.		
		TOTAL MARKETING COST	5012.	BANK LOAN BALANCE	0.
TOTAL OTHER COST	5448.	TOTAL OTHER COST	5448.		
TOTAL OTHER INCOME	20.	DIVIDENDS PAID	0.	BONDS OUTSTANDING	30000.
NET PROFIT BFOR TAXES	8575.	LOAN REPAYMENT	3000.		
		BONDS REDEEMED	0.	CAPITAL STOCK VALUE	63934.
INCOME TAXES	4288.	INCOME TAXES	4288.	ACCUM. RET. EARNINGS	6843.
PROFIT SHARING COST	0.	PROFIT SHARING COST	0.	TOTAL STOCK. EQUITY	70776.
NET INCOME	4288.	PLANT & EQUIP. INVEST.	4288.	TOTAL LIABILITIES	100776.
DIVIDENDS PAID	0.	SAVINGS ACCT. DEPOSIT	16.		
RETAINED EARNINGS	4288.	TOTAL DISBURSEMENTS	28861.		
		CASH AVAILABLE	3434.		
		EMERGENCY BANK LOAN	0.		
		CASH BALANCE	3434.		

5. ECONOMY AND STOCK MARKET

GROSS NATIONAL PRODUCT 175. ($BILLIONS)   PERSONAL CONSUMPTION EXP.--DURABLES   14. ($BILLIONS)
NUMBER OF HOUSEHOLD FORMATIONS 410. (1000.S)   RAW MATERIAL COST   0.35 ($/LB.)

COMPANY	STOCK PRICE	EARNINGS	SALES COMM.	PROFIT SHARING	DIVIDENDS	SHARES	PROD. WAGES	SALES SALARIES	BOND INTEREST	LOAN INTEREST
LOSSES UNLIMITED, INC.	10.66	0.71	0.31	0.0	0.0	6000.	5.18	996.	10.0	13.0
UNAWESOME FOURSOME ASSN.	10.66	0.71	0.31	0.0	0.0	6000.	5.13	989.	10.0	13.0
BOZO PRODUCTIONS	10.66	0.71	0.29	0.0	0.0	6000.	5.09	966.	10.0	13.0
DIVERSIFIED, INC.	10.66	0.71	0.31	0.0	0.0	6000.	4.80	977.	10.0	13.0
THE SYNDICATE	10.66	0.71	0.30	0.0	0.0	6000.	4.86	972.	10.0	13.0
THE BENDOKEMPF CORP.	10.66	0.71	0.32	0.0	0.0	6000.	5.08	947.	10.0	13.0
UNETHICAL, INC.	10.66	0.71	0.31	0.0	0.0	6000.	4.89	998.	10.0	13.0

6. INDUSTRY ESTIMATES

COMPANY	AVERAGE PRICE	AVERAGE ADVERT.	SALES FORCE	PROD. WORKFORCE	PROD. OUTPUT	UNIT SALES
LOSSES UNLIMITED, INC.	253.	264.	37	3009	163390	135097
UNAWESOME FOURSOME ASSN.	243.	254.	36	2906	161037	137617
BOZO PRODUCTIONS	254.	248.	38	3157	159268	137976
DIVERSIFIED, INC.	260.	254.	36	3014	161182	131663
THE SYNDICATE	248.	280.	38	3080	161025	141616
THE BENDOKEMPF CORP.	239.	265.	37	3044	162996	142278
UNETHICAL, INC.	262.	246.	39	2931	166079	142871

COMPANY 1 INDUSTRY 1 YEAR 1 QUARTER 3

1. DECISIONS

	MARKET 1	MARKET 2	MARKET 3
PRICE ($/UNIT)	275.	275.	250.
ADVERTISING ($1000/QTR.)	325.	300.	200.
SALES FORCE CHANGE (NO.)	0	0	0
PRODUCT R & D ($1000/QTR.)	40.		
SALES COMMISSION (%)	0.3		
PROFIT SHARING (%)	0.0		
SALES SALARIES ($/MONTH)	1000.		
SALES TRAINING ($1000/QTR.)	5.		
PRODUCTION TRAINING ($1000/QTR.)	6.		
PRODUCTION WAGES ($/HR.)	5.00		
PRODUCTION SCHEDULED (HOURS/WEEK)	40.		
LABOR FORCE CHANGE (NO.)	0		
ALLOCATION TO MARKETS (%)	35.	35.	30.
PROCESS R & D ($1000/QTR.)	40.		
RAW MATERIALS ORDERED (MILLION LBS.)	60.		
BONDS SOLD OR REDEEMED ($1000)	0.		
BANK LOAN REQUESTED ($1000)	4500.		
DIVIDENDS PAID ($1000)	0.		
STOCK ISSUED(1000 SHARES)	0.		
SAVINGS ACCOUNT ($1000)	0.		

2. PRODUCTION AND SALES

	MARKET 1	MARKET 2	MARKET 3	TOTAL
PRODUCTION WORKFORCE (NO.)	3010			
PRODUCTIVITY (UNITS/MAN-HOUR)	0.096			
RAW MATERIAL REQUIREMENTS (LBS./UNIT)	165.			
PRODUCTION OUTPUT (NO. OF UNITS)	52443	52443	44951	149837
FIN PROD INVENTORY (NO. UNITS)	44408	43581	59711	147700
RAW MAT INVENTORY (MILLION LBS.)	77.282			
DEMAND (NO. OF UNITS ORDERED)	63121	64022	41285	168428
SALES (NO. OF UNITS SOLD)	63121	64022	41285	168428
SALES ($1000)	17358.	17606.	10321.	45286.
SALESMEN ACTIVE (NO.)	17	17	9	43
SALES TRAINEES (NO.)	0	0	0	0

3. COSTS

PRODUCTION ($1000)

LABOR	7826.
MATERIAL	8663.
MAINTENANCE	1174.
TRAINING	6.
PROD LEVEL CHANGE	0.
EQUIPMENT	866.
ADMINISTRATIVE	1149.
DEPRECIATION	490.
TOTAL	20174.

MARKETING ($1000)

ADVERTISING	825.
SALARIES	129.
COMMISSIONS	136.
TRANSPORTATION	1221.
ADMINISTRATIVE	2772.
SALES FORCE CHANGE	0.
TRAINING	5.
TOTAL	5088.

OTHER ($1000)

R & D	80.
CARRYING-FIN PROD	665.
CARRYING-RAW MAT	168.
BOND INTEREST	750.
LOAN INTEREST	0.
ADMINISTRATIVE	4180.
BOND CALL PREMIUM	0.
TOTAL	5843.

118

4. FINANCIAL STATEMENTS

INCOME STATEMENT ($1000)		FLOW OF FUNDS STATEMENT ($1000)		FINANCIAL POSITION STATEMENT ($1000)	
GROSS SALES REVENUE	45286.	ACCOUNTS COLLECTED	41965.	CASH BALANCE	409.
BEGINNING INVENTORY	20836.	BANK LOANS REQUESTED	4500.	ACCOUNTS RECEIVABLE	15095.
TOTAL PRODUCTION COST	20174.	BOND SALE RETURN	0.	INVENTORY-FIN. PROD.	19748.
GOODS AVAILABLE	41010.	SAV ACCT-INT & WITHDRAWAL	20.	INVENTORY-RAB MAT.	27049.
ENDING INVENTORY	19748.	PLANT & EQUIP. SALE	0.	SAVINGS ACCT BALANCE	1000.
COST OF GOODS SOLD	21262.	STOCK SALE RETURN	0.	TOTAL CURRENT ASSETS	63302.
GROSS PROFIT	24024.	BEGINNING CASH	3434.		
		TOTAL SOURCES	49918.	PLANT & EQUIP. VALUE	48531.
TOTAL MARKETING COST	5088.			TOTAL ASSETS	111833.
PROFIT ON SALES	18936.	TOTAL PRODUCTION COST	32021.		
		TOTAL MARKETING COST	5088.	BANK LOAN BALANCE	4500.
TOTAL OTHER COST	5843.	TOTAL OTHER COST	5843.		
TOTAL OTHER INCOME	20.	DIVIDENDS PAID	0.	BONDS OUTSTANDING	30000.
NET PROFIT BFOR TAXES	13112.	LOAN REPAYMENT	0.		
		BONDS REDEEMED	0.	CAPITAL STOCK VALUE	63934.
INCOME TAXES	6556.	INCOME TAXES	6556.	ACCUM. RET. EARNINGS	13399.
PROFIT SHARING COST	0.	PROFIT SHARING COST	0.	TOTAL STOCK. EQUITY	77332.
NET INCOME	6556.	PLANT & EQUIP. INVEST.	6556.	TOTAL LIABILITIES	111833.
DIVIDENDS PAID	0.	SAVINGS ACCT. DEPOSIT	0.		
RETAINED EARNINGS	6556.	TOTAL DISBURSEMENTS	49509.		
		CASH AVAILABLE	409.		
		EMERGENCY BANK LOAN	0.		
		CASH BALANCE	409.		

5. ECONOMY AND STOCK MARKET

GROSS NATIONAL PRODUCT 131. ($BILLIONS)
NUMBER OF HOUSEHOLD FORMATIONS 411. (1000,S)

PERSONAL CONSUMPTION EXP.--DURABLES 15. ($BILLIONS)
RAW MATERIAL COST 0.31 ($/LB.)

COMPANY	STOCK PRICE	EARNINGS	SALES COMM.	DIVIDENDS	PROFIT SHARING	SALES SALARIES	PROD. WAGES	SHARES	BOND INTEREST	LOAN INTEREST
LOSSES UNLIMITED, INC.	10.66	1.09	0.28	0.0	0.0	956.	5.00	6000.	10.0	13.0
UNAWESOME FOURSOME ASSN.	10.66	1.09	0.29	0.0	0.0	1019.	4.96	6000.	10.0	13.0
BOZO PRODUCTIONS	10.66	1.09	0.30	0.0	0.0	1023.	5.09	6000.	10.0	13.0
DIVERSIFIED, INC.	10.66	1.09	0.31	0.0	0.0	1009.	4.97	6000.	10.0	13.0
THE SYNDICATE	10.66	1.09	0.31	0.0	0.0	1010.	5.22	6000.	10.0	13.0
THE BENDOKEMPF CORP.	10.66	1.09	0.30	0.0	0.0	991.	4.93	6000.	10.0	13.0
UNETHICAL, INC.	10.66	1.09	0.30	0.0	0.0	987.	4.94	6000.	10.0	13.0

6. INDUSTRY ESTIMATES

COMPANY	AVERAGE PRICE	AVERAGE ADVERT.	PROD. WORKFORCE	PROD. OUTPUT	SALES FORCE	UNIT SALES
LOSSES UNLIMITED, INC.	273.	282.	2824	146911	43	169779
UNAWESOME FOURSOME ASSN.	265.	278.	2938	144865	43	161138
BOZO PRODUCTIONS	260.	277.	2980	151388	45	168370
DIVERSIFIED, INC.	274.	270.	2949	149599	41	166990
THE SYNDICATE	264.	272.	3036	146441	44	166244
THE BENDOKEMPF CORP.	252.	275.	3068	149648	43	173109
UNETHICAL, INC.	274.	287.	2950	153697	44	166395

COMPANY 1   INDUSTRY 1   YEAR 1   QUARTER 4

1. DECISIONS

	MARKET 1	MARKET 2	MARKET 3
PRICE ($/UNIT)	275.	300.	250.
ADVERTISING ($1000/QTR.)	280.	280.	175.
SALES FORCE CHANGE (NO.)	0	0	0
PRODUCT R & D ($1000/QTR.)	40.		
SALES COMMISSION (%)	0.3		
PROFIT SHARING (%)	0.3		
SALES SALARIES ($/MONTH)	1000.		
SALES TRAINING ($1000/QTR)	15.		
PRODUCTION TRAINING ($1000/QTR.)	8.		
PRODUCTION WAGES ($/HR.)	5.00		
PRODUCTION SCHEDULED (HOURS/WEEK)	60.		
LABOR FORCE CHANGE (NO.)	0		
ALLOCATION TO MARKETS (%)	35.	40.	25.
PROCESS R & D ($1000/QTR.)	40.		
RAW MATERIALS ORDERED (MILLION LBS.)	0.		
BONDS SOLD OR REDEEMED ($1000)	0.		
BANK LOAN REQUESTED ($1000)	0.		
DIVIDENDS PAID ($1000)	0.		
STOCK ISSUED(1000 SHARES)	0.		
SAVINGS ACCOUNT ($1000)	0.		

2. PRODUCTION AND SALES

	MARKET 1	MARKET 2	MARKET 3	TOTAL
PRODUCTION WORKFORCE (NO.)	3010			
PRODUCTIVITY (UNITS/MAN-HOUR)	0.090			
RAW MATERIAL REQUIREMENTS (LBS./UNIT)	176.			
PRODUCTION OUTPUT (NO. OF UNITS)	73574	84084	52553	210211
FIN PROD INVENTORY (NO. UNITS)	54142	67740	73774	195656
RAW MAT INVENTORY (MILLION LBS.)	40.267			
DEMAND (NO. OF UNITS ORDERED)	63840	59925	38490	162255
SALES (NO. OF UNITS SOLD)	63840	59925	38490	162255
SALES ($1000)	17556.	17977.	9623.	45156.
SALESMEN ACTIVE (NO.)	17	17	9	43
SALES TRAINEES (NO.)	0	0	0	0

3. COSTS

PRODUCTION ($1000)

LABOR	13696.
MATERIAL	12955.
MAINTENANCE	2054.
TRAINING	8.
PROD LEVEL CHANGE	0.
EQUIPMENT	1296.
ADMINISTRATIVE	1451.
DEPRECIATION	485.

MARKETING ($1000)

ADVERTISING	735.
SALARIES	129.
COMMISSIONS	135.
TRANSPORTATION	1776.
ADMINISTRATIVE	2741.
SALES FORCE CHANGE	0.
TRAINING	15.

OTHER ($1000)

R & D	80.
CARRYING-FIN PROD	591.
CARRYING-RAW MAT	309.
BOND INTEREST	750.
LOAN INTEREST	146.
ADMINISTRATIVE	4174.
BOND CALL PREMIUM	0.

TOTAL   6050.

4. FINANCIAL STATEMENTS

INCOME STATEMENT ($1000)

GROSS SALES REVENUE	45156.
BEGINNING INVENTORY	19748.
TOTAL PRODUCTION COST	31945.
GOODS AVAILABLE	51693.
ENDING INVENTORY	29346.
COST OF GOODS SOLD	22348.
GROSS PROFIT	22808.
TOTAL MARKETING COST	5532.
PROFIT ON SALES	17276.
TOTAL OTHER COST	6050.
TOTAL OTHER INCOME	20.
NET PROFIT BFOR TAXES	11246.
INCOME TAXES	5623.
PROFIT SHARING COST	17.
NET INCOME	5606.
DIVIDENDS PAID	0.
RETAINED EARNINGS	5606.

FLOW OF FUNDS STATEMENT ($1000)

ACCOUNTS COLLECTED	45199.
BANK LOANS REQUESTED	0.
BOND SALE RETURN	0.
SAV ACCT-INT & WITHDRAWAL	20.
PLANT & EQUIP. SALE	0.
STOCK SALE RETURN	0.
BEGINNING CASH	409.
TOTAL SOURCES	45628.
TOTAL PRODUCTION COST	18504.
TOTAL MARKETING COST	5532.
TOTAL OTHER COST	6050.
DIVIDENDS PAID	0.
LOAN REPAYMENT	4500.
BONDS REDEEMED	0.
INCOME TAXES	5623.
PROFIT SHARING COST	17.
PLANT & EQUIP. INVEST.	0.
SAVINGS ACCT. DEPOSIT	0.
TOTAL DISBURSEMENTS	40226.
CASH AVAILABLE	5402.
EMERGENCY BANK LOAN	0.
CASH BALANCE	5402.

FINANCIAL POSITION STATEMENT ($1000)

CASH BALANCE	5402.
ACCOUNTS RECEIVABLE	15052.
INVENTORY-FIN. PROD.	29346.
INVENTORY-RAW MAT.	14094.
SAVINGS ACCT BALANCE	1000.
TOTAL CURRENT ASSETS	64893.
PLANT & EQUIP. VALUE	48046.
TOTAL ASSETS	112939.
BANK LOAN BALANCE	0.
BONDS OUTSTANDING	30000.
CAPITAL STOCK VALUE	63934.
ACCUM. RET. EARNINGS	19005.
TOTAL STOCK. EQUITY	82939.
TOTAL LIABILITIES	112939.

---

5. ECONOMY AND STOCK MARKET

GROSS NATIONAL PRODUCT	175. ($BILLIONS)	PERSONAL CONSUMPTION EXP.==DURABLES	11. ($BILLIONS)
NUMBER OF HOUSEHOLD FORMATIONS	408. (1000.S)	RAW MATERIAL COST	0.42 ($/LB.)

COMPANY	STOCK PRICE	EARNINGS	SALES COMM.	PROFIT SHARING	DIVIDENDS	SHARES	PROD. WAGES	SALES SALARIES	AVERAGE PRICE	AVERAGE ADVERT.	BOND INTEREST	LOAN INTEREST
LOSSES UNLIMITED, INC.	10.66	0.93	0.30	0.30	0.0	6000.	4.83	987.	265.	242.	10.0	13.0
UNAWESOME FOURSOME ASSN.	10.66	0.93	0.29	0.30	0.0	6000.	5.14	955.	278.	253.	10.0	13.0
BOZO PRODUCTIONS	10.66	0.93	0.29	0.32	0.0	6000.	4.94	1010.	279.	234.	10.0	13.0
DIVERSIFIED, INC.	10.66	0.93	0.31	0.29	0.0	6000.	4.85	1001.	287.	250.	10.0	13.0
THE SYNDICATE	10.66	0.93	0.30	0.31	0.0	6000.	5.19	1040.	277.	257.	10.0	13.0
THE BENDOKEMPF CORP.	10.66	0.93	0.31	0.29	0.0	6000.	5.36	995.	261.	235.	10.0	13.0
UNETHICAL, INC.	10.66	0.93	0.31	0.30	0.0	6000.	3.04	1021.	271.	235.	10.0	13.0

---

6. INDUSTRY ESTIMATES

COMPANY	AVERAGE PRICE	AVERAGE ADVERT.	SALES COMM.	PROFIT SHARING	SALES SALARIES	PROD. WAGES	PROD. WORKFORCE	PROD. OUTPUT	SALES FORCE	UNIT SALES
LOSSES UNLIMITED, INC.	265.	242.	0.30	0.30	987.	4.83	3018	207967	42	170477
UNAWESOME FOURSOME ASSN.	278.	253.	0.29	0.30	955.	5.14	3028	221638	43	159742
BOZO PRODUCTIONS	279.	234.	0.29	0.32	1010.	4.94	3141	200979	42	168657
DIVERSIFIED, INC.	287.	250.	0.31	0.29	1001.	4.85	3012	213621	45	154679
THE SYNDICATE	277.	257.	0.30	0.31	1040.	5.19	3037	216368	43	161909
THE BENDOKEMPF CORP.	261.	235.	0.31	0.29	995.	5.36	2991	212065	42	164725
UNETHICAL, INC.	271.	235.	0.31	0.30	1021.	3.04	3011	198357	42	164524

COMPANY 1   INDUSTRY 1   YEAR 2   QUARTER 1

1. DECISIONS

	MARKET 1	MARKET 2	MARKET 3
PRICE ($/UNIT)	300.	300.	275.
ADVERTISING ($1000/QTR.)	300.	300.	200.
SALES FORCE CHANGE (NO.)	2	3	0
PRODUCT R & D ($1000/QTR.)	40.		
SALES COMMISSION (%)	0.3		
PROFIT SHARING (%)	0.3		
SALES SALARIES ($/MONTH)	1250.		
SALES TRAINING ($1000/QTR.)	15.		
PRODUCTION TRAINING ($1000/QTR.)	8.		
PRODUCTION WAGES ($/HR.)	5.25		
PRODUCTION SCHEDULED (HOURS/WEEK)	45.		
LABOR FORCE CHANGE (NO.)	225.		
ALLOCATION TO MARKETS (%)	60.	40.	0.
PROCESS R & D ($1000/QTR.)	40.		
RAW MATERIALS ORDERED (MILLION LBS.)	70.		
BONDS SOLD OR REDEEMED ($1000)	0.		
BANK LOAN REQUESTED ($1000)	16000.		
DIVIDENDS PAID ($1000)	3000.		
STOCK ISSUED(1000 SHARES)	0.		
SAVINGS ACCOUNT ($1000)	0.		

2. PRODUCTION AND SALES

	MARKET 1	MARKET 2	MARKET 3	TOTAL
PRODUCTION WORKFORCE (NO.)	3235			
PRODUCTIVITY (UNITS/MAN-HOUR)	0.084			
RAW MATERIAL REQUIREMENTS (LBS./UNIT)	187.			
PRODUCTION OUTPUT (NO. OF UNITS)	95480	63653	0	159133
FIN PROD INVENTORY (NO. OF UNITS)	96101	81599	42701	220401
RAW MAT INVENTORY (MILLION LBS.)	80.452			
DEMAND (NO. OF UNITS ORDERED)	53521	49794	31073	134388
SALES (NO. OF UNITS SOLD)	53521	49794	31073	134388
SALES ($1000)	16056.	14938.	8545.	39540.
SALESMEN ACTIVE (NO.)	17	17	9	43
SALES TRAINEES (NO.)	2	3	0	5

3. COSTS

PRODUCTION ($1000)		MARKETING ($1000)		OTHER ($1000)	
LABOR	10487.	ADVERTISING	800.	R & D	80.
MATERIAL	10435.	SALARIES	180.	CARRYING-FIN PROD	783.
MAINTENANCE	1573.	COMMISSIONS	119.	CARRYING-RAW MAT	161.
TRAINING	8.	TRANSPORTATION	1464.	BOND INTEREST	750.
PROD LEVEL CHANGE	226.	ADMINISTRATIVE	2652.	LOAN INTEREST	0.
EQUIPMENT	1044.	SALES FORCE CHANGE	42.	ADMINISTRATIVE	3962.
ADMINISTRATIVE	1196.	TRAINING	15.	BOND CALL PREMIUM	0.
DEPRECIATION	480.				
		TOTAL	5272.	TOTAL	5736.

4. FINANCIAL STATEMENTS

INCOME STATEMENT ($1000)

GROSS SALES REVENUE	39540.
BEGINNING INVENTORY	29346.
TOTAL PRODUCTION COST	25449.
GOODS AVAILABLE	54795.
ENDING INVENTORY	34639.
COST OF GOODS SOLD	20156.
GROSS PROFIT	19383.
TOTAL MARKETING COST	5272.
PROFIT ON SALES	14112.
TOTAL OTHER COST	5736.
TOTAL OTHER INCOME	20.
NET PROFIT BFOR TAXES	8735.
INCOME TAXES	4367.
PROFIT SHARING COST	13.
NET INCOME	4354.
DIVIDENDS PAID	3000.
RETAINED EARNINGS	1354.

FLOW OF FUNDS STATEMENT ($1000)

ACCOUNTS COLLECTED	41412.
BANK LOANS REQUESTED	16000.
BOND SALE RETURN	0.
SAV ACCT-INT & WITHDRAWAL	20.
PLANT & EQUIP. SALE	0.
STOCK SALE RETURN	0.
BEGINNING CASH	5402.
TOTAL SOURCES	62834.
TOTAL PRODUCTION COST	43934.
TOTAL MARKETING COST	5272.
TOTAL OTHER COST	5736.
DIVIDENDS PAID	3000.
LOAN REPAYMENT	0.
BONDS REDEEMED	0.
INCOME TAXES	4367.
PROFIT SHARING COST	13.
PLANT & EQUIP. INVEST.	339.
SAVINGS ACCT. DEPOSIT	0.
TOTAL DISBURSEMENTS	62660.
CASH AVAILABLE	174.
EMERGENCY BANK LOAN	0.
CASH BALANCE	174.

FINANCIAL POSITION STATEMENT ($1000)

CASH BALANCE	174.
ACCOUNTS RECEIVABLE	13180.
INVENTORY-FIN. PROD.	34639.
INVENTORY-RAW MAT.	33058.
SAVINGS ACCT BALANCE	1000.
TOTAL CURRENT ASSETS	82051.
PLANT & EQUIP. VALUE	47904.
TOTAL ASSETS	129954.
BANK LOAN BALANCE	16000.
BONDS OUTSTANDING	30000.
CAPITAL STOCK VALUE	63595.
ACCUM. RET. EARNINGS	20359.
TOTAL STOCK. EQUITY	83954.
TOTAL LIABILITIES	129954.

5. ECONOMY AND STOCK MARKET

GROSS NATIONAL PRODUCT 141. ($BILLIONS)
NUMBER OF HOUSEHOLD FORMATIONS 401. (1000.S)

PERSONAL CONSUMPTION EXP.--DURABLES 12. ($BILLIONS)
RAW MATERIAL COST 0.46 ($/LB.)

COMPANY	STOCK PRICE	EARNINGS	DIVIDENDS	SHARES	BOND INTEREST	LOAN INTEREST
LOSSES UNLIMITED, INC.	10.60	0.73	0.50	6000.	10.0	13.0
UNAWESOME FOURSOME ASSN.	10.60	0.73	0.50	6000.	10.0	13.0
BOZO PRODUCTIONS	10.60	0.73	0.50	6000.	10.0	13.0
DIVERSIFIED, INC.	10.60	0.73	0.50	6000.	10.0	13.0
THE SYNDICATE	10.60	0.73	0.50	6000.	10.0	13.0
THE BENDOKEMPF CORP.	10.60	0.73	0.50	6000.	10.0	13.0
UNETHICAL, INC.	10.60	0.73	0.50	6000.	10.0	13.0

6. INDUSTRY ESTIMATES

COMPANY	AVERAGE PRICE	AVERAGE ADVERT.	SALES COMM.	PROFIT SHARING	SALES SALARIES	PROD. WAGES	PROD. WORKFORCE	PROD. OUTPUT	SALES FORCE	UNIT SALES
LOSSES UNLIMITED, INC.	290.	269.	0.31	0.29	1268.	5.31	3266	164543	41	136477
UNAWESOME FOURSOME ASSN.	296.	262.	0.30	0.30	1335.	5.21	3216	158827	44	133084
BOZO PRODUCTIONS	280.	259.	0.30	0.30	1261.	5.08	3254	158810	42	134916
DIVERSIFIED, INC.	279.	276.	0.31	0.30	1282.	5.36	3301	160102	43	142941
THE SYNDICATE	298.	267.	0.32	0.30	1226.	5.10	3317	151391	43	141700
THE BENDOKEMPF CORP.	289.	269.	0.31	0.31	1249.	5.09	3185	156816	41	135092
UNETHICAL, INC.	293.	255.	0.32	0.30	1275.	5.33	3090	149440	43	133770

COMPANY 1   INDUSTRY 1   YEAR 2   QUARTER 2

1. DECISIONS

	MARKET 1	MARKET 2	MARKET 3
PRICE ($/UNIT)	300.	325.	275.
ADVERTISING ($1000/QTR.)	330.	330.	250.
SALES FORCE CHANGE (NO.)	3	4	0
PRODUCT R & D ($1000/QTR.)	40.		
SALES COMMISSION (%)	0.3		
PROFIT SHARING (%)	0.3		
SALES SALARIES ($/MONTH)	1250.		
SALES TRAINING ($1000/QTR.)	15.		
PRODUCTION TRAINING ($1000/QTR.)	12.		
PRODUCTION WAGES ($/HR.)	5.25		
PRODUCTION SCHEDULED (HOURS/WEEK)	40.		
LABOR FORCE CHANGE (NO.)	115		
ALLOCATION TO MARKETS (%)	40.	45.	15.
PROCESS R & D ($1000/QTR.)	40.		
RAW MATERIALS ORDERED (MILLION LBS.)	0.		
BONDS SOLD OR REDEEMED ($1000)	0.		
BANK LOAN REQUESTED ($1000)	4000.		
DIVIDENDS PAID ($1000)	3000.		
STOCK ISSUED(1000 SHARES)	0.		
SAVINGS ACCOUNT ($1000)	0.		

2. PRODUCTION AND SALES

	MARKET 1	MARKET 2	MARKET 3	TOTAL
PRODUCTION WORKFORCE (NO.)	3350			
PRODUCTIVITY (UNITS/MAN-HOUR)	0.079			
RAW MATERIAL REQUIREMENTS (LBS./UNIT)	199.			
PRODUCTION OUTPUT (NO. OF UNITS)	54765	61611	20537	136913
FIN PROD INVENTORY (NO. UNITS)	82163	84306	25142	191611
RAW MAT INVENTORY (MILLION LBS.)	53.195			
DEMAND (NO. OF UNITS ORDERED)	68703	58904	38096	165703
SALES (NO. OF UNITS SOLD)	68703	58904	38096	165703
SALES ($1000)	20611.	19144.	10476.	50231.
SALESMEN ACTIVE (NO.)	19	20	9	48
SALES TRAINEES (NO.)	3	4	0	7

3. COSTS

PRODUCTION ($1000)		MARKETING ($1000)		OTHER ($1000)	
LABOR	9146.	ADVERTISING	910.	R & D	80.
MATERIAL	11200.	SALARIES	206.	CARRYING-FIN PROD	882.
MAINTENANCE	1372.	COMMISSIONS	151.	CARRYING-RAW MAT	322.
TRAINING	12.	TRANSPORTATION	1219.	BOND INTEREST	750.
PROD LEVEL CHANGE	116.	ADMINISTRATIVE	2879.	LOAN INTEREST	520.
EQUIPMENT	1120.	SALES FORCE CHANGE	58.	ADMINISTRATIVE	4533.
ADMINISTRATIVE	1085.	TRAINING	15.	BOND CALL PREMIUM	0.
DEPRECIATION	479.				
TOTAL	24529.	TOTAL	5437.	TOTAL	7086.

4. FINANCIAL STATEMENTS

INCOME STATEMENT ($1000)

GROSS SALES REVENUE	50231.
BEGINNING INVENTORY	34639.
TOTAL PRODUCTION COST	24529.
GOODS AVAILABLE	59167.
ENDING INVENTORY	33125.
COST OF GOODS SOLD	26042.
GROSS PROFIT	24189.
TOTAL MARKETING COST	5437.
PROFIT ON SALES	18752.
TOTAL OTHER COST	7086.
TOTAL OTHER INCOME	20.
NET PROFIT BFOR TAXES	11859.
INCOME TAXES	5930.
PROFIT SHARING COST	18.
NET INCOME	5912.
DIVIDENDS PAID	3000.
RETAINED EARNINGS	2912.

FLOW OF FUNDS STATEMENT ($1000)

ACCOUNTS COLLECTED	46667.
BANK LOANS REQUESTED	4000.
BOND SALE RETURN	0.
SAV ACCT-INT & WITHDRAWAL	20.
PLANT & EQUIP. SALE	0.
STOCK SALE RETURN	0.
BEGINNING CASH	174.
TOTAL SOURCES	50861.
TOTAL PRODUCTION COST	12850.
TOTAL MARKETING COST	5437.
TOTAL OTHER COST	7086.
DIVIDENDS PAID	3000.
LOAN REPAYMENT	16000.
BONDS REDEEMED	0.
INCOME TAXES	5930.
PROFIT SHARING COST	18.
PLANT & EQUIP. INVEST.	174.
SAVINGS ACCT. DEPOSIT	0.
TOTAL DISBURSEMENTS	50494.
CASH AVAILABLE	367.
EMERGENCY BANK LOAN	0.
CASH BALANCE	367.

FINANCIAL POSITION STATEMENT ($1000)

CASH BALANCE	367.
ACCOUNTS RECEIVABLE	16744.
INVENTORY-FIN. PROD.	0.
INVENTORY-RAB MAT.	21858.
SAVINGS ACCT BALANCE	1000.
TOTAL CURRENT ASSETS	73094.
PLANT & EQUIP. VALUE	47599.
TOTAL ASSETS	120693.
BANK LOAN BALANCE	4000.
BONDS OUTSTANDING	30000.
CAPITAL STOCK VALUE	63421.
ACCUM. RET. EARNINGS	23271.
TOTAL STOCK. EQUITY	86692.
TOTAL LIABILITIES	120693.

5. ECONOMY AND STOCK MARKET

GROSS NATIONAL PRODUCT   188. ($BILLIONS)
NUMBER OF HOUSEHOLD FORMATIONS   386. (1000.S)

PERSONAL CONSUMPTION EXP.--DURABLES   17. ($BILLIONS)
RAB MATERIAL COST   0.42 ($/LB.)

COMPANY	STOCK PRICE	EARNINGS	SALES COMM.	AVERAGE ADVERT.	AVERAGE PRICE	PROFIT SHARING	DIVIDENDS	SHARES	BOND INTEREST	LOAN INTEREST
LOSSES UNLIMITED, INC.	10.57	0.99	0.30	301.	296.	0.30	0.50	6000.	10.0	13.0
UNAWESOME FOURSOME ASSN.	10.57	0.99	0.30	308.	283.	0.31	0.50	6000.	10.0	13.0
BOZO PRODUCTIONS	10.57	0.99	0.30	299.	298.	0.31	0.50	6000.	10.0	13.0
DIVERSIFIED, INC.	10.57	0.99	0.31	301.	307.	0.30	0.50	6000.	10.0	13.0
THE SYNDICATE	10.57	0.99	0.29	296.	308.	0.32	0.50	6000.	10.0	13.0
THE BENDOKEMPF CORP.	10.57	0.99	0.30	311.	308.	0.29	0.50	6000.	10.0	13.0
UNETHICAL, INC.	10.57	0.99	0.31	315.	318.	0.31	0.50	6000.	10.0	13.0

6. INDUSTRY ESTIMATES

COMPANY	SALES SALARIES	PROD. WAGES	PROD. WORKFCRCE	PROD. OUTPUT	SALES FORCE	UNIT SALES
LOSSES UNLIMITED, INC.	1287.	5.13	3434	138047	48	165817
UNAWESOME FOURSOME ASSN.	1249.	5.04	3373	132880	49	167306
BOZO PRODUCTIONS	1251.	5.06	3270	139809	50	159068
DIVERSIFIED, INC.	1282.	5.26	3236	131359	48	161461
THE SYNDICATE	1256.	5.41	3132	128008	49	165271
THE BENDOKEMPF CORP.	1201.	5.20	3359	140179	48	175828
UNETHICAL, INC.	1216.	5.08	3131	134857	47	152731

COMPANY 1   INDUSTRY 1   YEAR 2   QUARTER 3

1. DECISIONS

	MARKET 1	MARKET 2	MARKET 3
PRICE ($/UNIT)	325.	325.	300.
ADVERTISING ($1000/QTR.)	350.	350.	275.
SALES FORCE CHANGE (NO.)	0	0	0
PRODUCT R & D ($1000/QTR.)	40.		
SALES COMMISSION (%)	0.3		
PROFIT SHARING (%)	0.3		
SALES SALARIES ($/MONTH)	1250.		
SALES TRAINING ($1000/QTR.)	20.		
PRODUCTION TRAINING ($1000/QTR.)	12.		
PRODUCTION WAGES ($/HR.)	5.25		
PRODUCTION SCHEDULED (HOURS/WEEK)	40.		
LABOR FORCE CHANGE (NO.)	250		
ALLOCATION TO MARKETS (%)	43.	37.	20.
PROCESS R & D ($1000/QTR.)	40.		
RAW MATERIALS ORDERED (MILLION LBS.)	70.		
BONDS SOLD OR REDEEMED ($1000)	0.		
BANK LOAN REQUESTED ($1000)	15000.		
DIVIDENDS PAID ($1000)	3000.		
STOCK ISSUED(1000 SHARES)	0.		
SAVINGS ACCOUNT ($1000)	0.		

2. PRODUCTION AND SALES

	MARKET 1	MARKET 2	MARKET 3	TOTAL
PRODUCTION WORKFORCE (NO.)	3600			
PRODUCTIVITY (UNITS/MAN-HOUR)	0.074			
RAW MATERIAL REQUIREMENTS (LBS./UNIT)	211.			
PRODUCTION OUTPUT (NC. OF UNITS)	59562	51251	27703	138516
FIN PROD INVENTORY (NO. UNITS)	66749	71799	10939	149487
RAW MAT INVENTORY (MILLION LBS.)	93.924			
DEMAND (NO. OF UNITS ORDERED)	74976	63758	41906	180640
SALES (NO. OF UNITS SOLD)	74976	63758	41906	180640
SALES ($1000)	24367.	20721.	12572.	57660.
SALESMEN ACTIVE (NO.)	22	24	9	55
SALES TRAINEES (NO.)	0	0	0	0

3. COSTS

PRODUCTION ($1000)

LABOR	9828.
MATERIAL	12028.
MAINTENANCE	1474.
TRAINING	12.
PROD LEVEL CHANGE	251.
EQUIPMENT	1203.
ADMINISTRATIVE	1093.
DEPRECIATION	476.
TOTAL	?6?6?

MARKETING ($1000)

ADVERTISING	975.
SALARIES	206.
COMMISSIONS	173.
TRANSPORTATION	1179.
ADMINISTRATIVE	2953.
SALES FORCE CHANGE	0.
TRAINING	20.
TOTAL	5506.

OTHER ($1000)

R & D	80.
CARRYING-FIN PROD	766.
CARRYING-RAW MAT	213.
BOND INTEREST	750.
LOAN INTEREST	130.
ADMINISTRATIVE	4980.
BOND CALL PREMIUM	0.
TOTAL	6919.

4. FINANCIAL STATEMENTS

INCOME STATEMENT ($1000)

GROSS SALES REVENUE	57660.
BEGINNING INVENTORY	33125.
TOTAL PRODUCTION COST	26364.
GOODS AVAILABLE	59489.
ENDING INVENTORY	27968.
COST OF GOODS SOLD	31521.
GROSS PROFIT	26139.
TOTAL MARKETING COST	5506.
PROFIT ON SALES	20633.
TOTAL OTHER COST	6919.
TOTAL OTHER INCOME	20.
NET PROFIT BFOR TAXES	14110.
INCOME TAXES	7055.
PROFIT SHARING COST	21.
NET INCOME	7034.
DIVIDENDS PAID	3000.
RETAINED EARNINGS	4034.

FLOW OF FUNDS STATEMENT ($1000)

ACCOUNTS COLLECTED	55184.
BANK LOANS REQUESTED	15000.
BOND SALE RETURN	0.
SAV ACCT-INT & WITHDRAWAL	20.
PLANT & EQUIP. SALE	0.
STOCK SALE RETURN	0.
BEGINNING CASH	367.
TOTAL SOURCES	70571.
TOTAL PRODUCTION COST	43260.
TOTAL MARKETING COST	5506.
TOTAL OTHER COST	6919.
DIVIDENDS PAID	3000.
LOAN REPAYMENT	4000.
BONDS REDEEMED	0.
INCOME TAXES	7055.
PROFIT SHARING COST	21.
PLANT & EQUIP. INVEST.	7034.
SAVINGS ACCT. DEPOSIT	0.
TOTAL DISBURSEMENTS	70138.
CASH AVAILABLE	433.
EMERGENCY BANK LOAN	0.
CASH BALANCE	433.

FINANCIAL POSITION STATEMENT ($1000)

CASH BALANCE	433.
ACCOUNTS RECEIVABLE	19220.
INVENTORY-FIN. PROD.	27968.
INVENTORY-RAW MAT.	39230.
SAVINGS ACCT BALANCE	1000.
TOTAL CURRENT ASSETS	87852.
PLANT & EQUIP. VALUE	47499.
TOTAL ASSETS	135350.
BANK LOAN BALANCE	15000.
BONDS OUTSTANDING	30000.
CAPITAL STOCK VALUE	63045.
ACCUM. RET. EARNINGS	27305.
TOTAL STOCK. EQUITY	90350.
TOTAL LIABILITIES	135350.

5. ECONOMY AND STOCK MARKET

GROSS NATIONAL PRODUCT 126. ($BILLIONS) PERSONAL CONSUMPTION EXP.--DURABLES 18. ($BILLIONS)
NUMBER OF HOUSEHOLD FORMATIONS 391. (1000.S) RAW MATERIAL COST 0.39 ($/LB.)

COMPANY	STOCK PRICE	EARNINGS	SALES COMM.	PROFIT SHARING	DIVIDENDS	SALES SALARIES	SHARES	PROD. WAGES	BOND INTEREST	LOAN INTEREST
LOSSES UNLIMITED, INC.	10.51	1.17	0.29	0.30	0.50	1202.	6000.	5.03	10.0	13.0
UNAWESOME FOURSOME ASSN.	10.51	1.17	0.30	0.30	0.50	1194.	6000.	5.46	10.0	13.0
BOZO PRODUCTIONS	10.51	1.17	0.30	0.30	0.50	1284.	6000.	5.34	10.0	13.0
DIVERSIFIED, INC.	10.51	1.17	0.31	0.29	0.50	1242.	6000.	5.26	10.0	13.0
THE SYNDICATE	10.51	1.17	0.33	0.29	0.50	1330.	6000.	5.69	10.0	13.0
THE BENDOKEMPF CORP.	10.51	1.17	0.31	0.31	0.50	1256.	6000.	5.16	10.0	13.0
UNETHICAL, INC.	10.51	1.17	0.30	0.29	0.50	1250.	6000.	5.37	10.0	13.0

6. INDUSTRY ESTIMATES

COMPANY	AVERAGE PRICE	AVERAGE ADVERT.	PROD. WORKFORCE	PROD. OUTPUT	SALES FORCE	UNIT SALES
LOSSES UNLIMITED, INC.	318.	317.	3748	139385	52	178056
UNAWESOME FOURSOME ASSN.	319.	307.	3605	140024	54	183534
BOZO PRODUCTIONS	307.	325.	3603	140391	56	174942
DIVERSIFIED, INC.	312.	325.	3624	142214	52	178432
THE SYNDICATE	284.	318.	3616	138082	56	188597
THE BENDOKEMPF CORP.	310.	330.	3583	140015	55	178623
UNETHICAL, INC.	327.	324.	3673	141544	54	180911

COMPANY 1   INDUSTRY 1   YEAR 2   QUARTER 4

1. DECISIONS

	MARKET1	MARKET 2	MARKET 3
PRICE ($/UNIT)	300.	300.	300.
ADVERTISING ($1000/QTR.)	300.	300.	300.
SALES FORCE CHANGE (NO.)	2	0	3
PRODUCT R & D ($100/QTR.)	50.		
SALES COMMISSION (X)	0.4		
PROFIT SHARING (%)	0.3		
SALES SALARIES ($/MONTH)	1500.		
SALES TRAINING ($1000/QTR.)	25.		
PRODUCTION TRAINING ($1000/QTR.)	15.		
PRODUCTION WAGES ($/HR.)	5.50		
PRODUCTION SCHEDULED (HOURS/WEEK)	40.		
LABOR FORCE CHANGE (NO.)	400		
ALLOCATION TO MARKETS (%)	43.	37.	20.
PROCESS R & D ($1000/QTR.)	40.		
RAW MATERIALS ORDERED (MILLION LBS.)	0.		
BONDS SOLD OR REDEEMED ($1000)	0.		
BANK LOAN REQUESTED ($1000)	0.		
DIVIDENDS PAID ($1000)	1692.		
STOCK ISSUED $1000 SHARES	0.		
SAVINGS ACCOUNT ($1000)	1500.		

2. PRODUCTION AND SALES

	MARKET1	MARKET 2	MARKET 3
PRODUCTION WORKFORCE (NO.)	4000		
PRODUCTIVITY (UNITS/MAN-HOUR)	0.069		
RAW MATERIAL REQUIREMENTS (LBS.UNITS)	224.		
PRODUCTION OUTPUT (NO. OF UNITS)	62081	53419	28875
FIN PROD INVENTORY (NO. UNITS)	22363	55555	2243
RAW MAT INVENTORY (MILLION LBS.)	62.454		
DEMAND (NO. OF UNITS ORDERED)	68185	67272	54537
SALES (NO. OF UNITS SOLD)	68185	67272	54537
SALES ($1000)	20456.	20181	16361
SALESMEN ACTIVE (NO.)	22	24	24
SALES TRAINEES (NO.)	2	0	3

3. COSTS

PRODUCTION ($1000)

LABOR	11440.
MATERIAL	13509.
MAINTENANCE	1716.
TRAINING	15.
PROD LEVEL CHANGE	401.
EQUIPMENT	1351.
ADMINISTRATIVE	1122.
DEPRECIATION	475.
TOTAL	30028.

MARKETING ($1000)

ADVERTISING	900.
SALARIES	270.
COMMISSIONS	207.
TRANSPORTATION	1229.
ADMINISTRATIVE	2963.
SALES FORCE CHANGE	42.
TRAINING	25.
TOTAL	5636.

OTHER ($1000)

R & D	90.
CARRYING-FIN PRCD	598.
CARRYING-RAW MAT	376.
BOND INTEREST	750.
LOAN INTEREST	488.
ADMINISTRATIVE	4807.
BOND CALL PREMIUM	0.
TOTAL	7109.

COMPANY 1 INDUSTRY 1 YEAR 2 QUARTER 4

4. FINANCIAL STATEMENTS

INCOME STATEMENT ($1000)

GROSS SALES REVENUE	56998.
BEGINNING INVENTORY	27968.
TOTAL PRODUCTION COST	30028.
GOODS AVAILABLE	57996.
ENDING INVENTORY	16690.
COST OF GOODS SOLD	41306.
GROSS PROFIT	15692
TOTAL MARKETING COST	5636.
PROFIT ON SALES	10056.
TOTAL OTHER COST	7109.
TOTAL OTHER INCOME	20.
NET PROFIT BEFORE TAXES	2967.
INCOME TAXES	1483.
PROFIT SHARING COST	4.
NET INCOME	1479.
DIVIDENDS PAID	1692.
RETAINED EARNINGS	-213.

(handwritten: 4.10.09 ; 352.68)

FLOW OF FUNDS STATEMENT ($1000)

ACCOUNTS COLLECTED	57238.
BANK LOANS REQUESTED	0.
BOND SALES RETURN	0.
SAV ACCT-INT & WITHDRAWAL	20.
PLANT & EQUIP. SALES	0.
STOCK SALE RETURN	0.
BEGINNING CASH	433.
TOTAL SOURCES	57691.
TOTAL PRODUCTION COST	15520.
TOTAL MARKETING COST	5636.
TOTAL OTHER COST	7109.
DIVIDENDS PAID	1692.
LOAN REPAYMENT	15000.
BONDS REDEEMED	0.
INCOME TAXES	1483.
PROFIT SHARING COST	4.
PLANT & EQUIP. INVEST.	601.
SAVINGS ACCT. DEPOSIT	1500.
TOTAL DISBURSEMENTS	48545.
CASH AVAILABLE	9146.
EMERGENCY BANK LOAN	0.
CASH BALANCE	9146.

FINANCIAL POSITION STATEMENT ($1000)

CASH BALANCE	9146.
ACCOUNTS RECEIVABLE	18999.
INVENTORY-FIN. PROD.	16690.
INVENTORY-RAW MAT.	26082.
SAVINGS ACCT BALANCE	2500.
TOTAL CURRENT ASSETS	73417.
PLANT & EQUIP. VALUE	47625.
TOTAL ASSETS	121042.
BANK LOAN BALANCE	0.
BONDS OUTSTANDING	30000.
CAPITAL STOCK VALUE	63950.
ACCUM. RET. EARNINGS	27092.
TOTAL STOCK. EQUITY	91042.
TOTAL LIABILITIES	121042.

5. ECONOMY AND STOCK MARKET

GROSS NATIONAL PRODUCT 173. ($BILLIONS)
NUMBER OF HOUSEHOLD FORMATIONS 383. (1000.S)
PERSONAL CONSUMPTION EXP--DURABLES 13. ($BILLIONS)
RAW MATERIAL COST 0.49 ($/LB.)

COMPANY	STOCK PRICE	EARNINGS	AVERAGE ADVERT.	SALES COMM.	DIVIDENDS	PROFIT SHARING	SALES SALARIES	SHARES	BOND INTEREST	LOAN INTEREST
LOSSES UNLIMITED, INC.	10.65	-.04	288.	0.39	0.28	0.30	1485.	6000.	10.0	13.0
UNAWESOME FOURSOME ASSN.	10.65	-.04	304.	0.41	0.28	0.29	1453.	6000.	10.0	13.0
BOZO PRODUCTIONS	10.65	-.04	299.	0.40	0.28	0.30	1419.	6000.	10.0	13.0
DIVERSIFIED, INC.	10.65	-.04	296.	0.40	0.28	0.30	1423.	6000.	10.0	13.0
THE SYNDICATE	10.65	-.04	315.	0.40	0.28	0.30	1564.	6000.	10.0	13.0
THE BENDOKEMPF CORP.	10.65	-.04	312.	0.42	0.28	0.28	1458.	6000.	10.0	13.0
UNETHICAL, INC.	10.65	-.04	301.	0.39	0.28	0.30	1491.	6000.	10.0	13.0

6. INDUSTRY ESTIMATES

COMPANY	AVERAGE PRICE	PROD. WAGES	PROD. WORKFORCE	PROD. OUTPUT	SALES FORCE	UNIT SALES
LOSSES UNLIMITED, INC.	312.	5.65	3790	139474	52	170111
UNAWESOME FOURSOME ASSN.	312.	5.45	4158	144157	55	169906
BOZO PRODUCTIONS	306.	5.59	3831	141421	53	182302
DIVERSIFIED, INC.	319.	5.64	3957	141646	53	163998
THE SYNDICATE	287.	5.55	3856	141895	56	169502
THE BENDOKEMPF CORP.	299.	5.70	3999	147032	54	177980
UNETHICAL, INC.	290.	5.66	4078	143191	57	173682

Appendix B
BUSPOG Blank Forms

2 Marketing Plan Forms
6 Sales Forecast Forms
2 Production Plan Forms
2 Raw Material Plan Forms
2 Human Resources Plan Forms
2 Wage and Salary Plan Forms
2 Cash Budget Forms
2 Cost Estimates Forms
2 Income Statement Forms
2 Position Statement Forms
4 Quarterly Decision Sheets

Marketing Plan Form

	Marketing Decisions	Year 2 Qtr. 1	Qtr. 2	Qtr. 3	Qtr. 4	Year 3	Year 4
1	Product Price - Mkt. 1 (in dollars)						
2	Product Price - Mkt. 2						
3	Product Price - Mkt. 3						
4	Advertising - Mkt.1 (in thousands of dollars)						
5	Advertising - Mkt.2						
6	Advertising - Mkt.3						
7	Salespersons - Mkt. 1						
8	Salespersons - Mkt. 2						
9	Salespersons - Mkt. 3						
10	Product R & D (in thousands of dollars)						
11	Sales Commission (in percent)						
Forecasted Sales							
12	Sales in - Market 1 Units						
13	Market 2						
14	Market 3						
15	Total						
16	Sales in Market 1 Dollars						
17	Market 2						
18	Market 3						
19	Total						

Marketing Plan Form

	Marketing Decisions	Year 2 Qtr. 1	Qtr. 2	Qtr. 3	Qtr. 4	Year 3	Year 4
1	Product Price - Mkt. 1 (in dollars)						
2	Product Price - Mkt. 2						
3	Product Price - Mkt. 3						
4	Advertising - Mkt.1 (in thousands of dollars)						
5	Advertising - Mkt.2						
6	Advertising - Mkt.3						
7	Salespersons - Mkt. 1						
8	Salespersons - Mkt. 2						
9	Salespersons - Mkt. 3						
10	Product R & D (in thousands of dollars)						
11	Sales Commission (in percent)						
Forecasted Sales							
12	Sales in - Market 1 Units						
13	Market 2						
14	Market 3						
15	Total						
16	Sales in Market 1 Dollars						
17	Market 2						
18	Market 3						
19	Total						

Sales Forecast Form

Market _____

(figures expressed in units)

		Year ____				Year ___	Year ___
		Qtr. 1	Qtr. 2	Qtr. 3	Qtr. 4	Total	Total
1	Previous Quarter Sales						
2	Previous Quarter Demand						
3	Customer Change						
4	Backorders						
5	Trend						
6	Seasonal						
7	Gross Domestic Prod.						
8	Pers. Consump. Exp.						
9	Household Forma.						
10	Price						
11	Advertising						
12	Sales Force Chg.						
13	Product R & D						
14	Sales Commission						
15	Sales Training						
16	Profit Sharing						
17	Total Adjustments						
18	Forecasted Demand						
19	Stockout Effect						
20	Forecasted Sales						

Sales Forecast Form

Market _____

(figures expressed in units)

		Year _____				Year ___	Year ___
		Qtr. 1	Qtr. 2	Qtr. 3	Qtr. 4	Total	Total
1	Previous Quarter Sales						
2	Previous Quarter Demand						
3	Customer Change						
4	Backorders						
5	Trend						
6	Seasonal						
7	Gross Domestic Prod.						
8	Pers. Consump. Exp.						
9	Household Forma.						
10	Price						
11	Advertising						
12	Sales Force Chg.						
13	Product R & D						
14	Sales Commission						
15	Sales Training						
16	Profit Sharing						
17	Total Adjustments						
18	Forecasted Demand						
19	Stockout Effect						
20	Forecasted Sales						

Sales Forecast Form

Market _____

(figures expressed in units)

		Year ____				Year ___	Year ___
		Qtr. 1	Qtr. 2	Qtr. 3	Qtr. 4	Total	Total
1	Previous Quarter Sales						
2	Previous Quarter Demand						
3	Customer Change						
4	Backorders						
5	Trend						
6	Seasonal						
7	Gross Domestic Prod.						
8	Pers. Consump. Exp.						
9	Household Forma.						
10	Price						
11	Advertising						
12	Sales Force Chg.						
13	Product R & D						
14	Sales Commission						
15	Sales Training						
16	Profit Sharing						
17	Total Adjustments						
18	Forecasted Demand						
19	Stockout Effect						
20	Forecasted Sales						

Sales Forecast Form

Market _____

(figures expressed in units)

		Year ____				Year ___	Year ___
		Qtr. 1	Qtr. 2	Qtr. 3	Qtr. 4	Total	Total
1	Previous Quarter Sales						
2	Previous Quarter Demand						
3	Customer Change						
4	Backorders						
5	Trend						
6	Seasonal						
7	Gross Domestic Prod.						
8	Pers. Consump. Exp.						
9	Household Forma.						
10	Price						
11	Advertising						
12	Sales Force Chg.						
13	Product R & D						
14	Sales Commission						
15	Sales Training						
16	Profit Sharing						
17	Total Adjustments						
18	Forecasted Demand						
19	Stockout Effect						
20	Forecasted Sales						

Sales Forecast Form

Market _____

(figures expressed in units)

		Year _____				Year ___	Year ___
		Qtr. 1	Qtr. 2	Qtr. 3	Qtr. 4	Total	Total
1	Previous Quarter Sales						
2	Previous Quarter Demand						
3	Customer Change						
4	Backorders						
5	Trend						
6	Seasonal						
7	Gross Domestic Prod.						
8	Pers. Consump. Exp.						
9	Household Forma.						
10	Price						
11	Advertising						
12	Sales Force Chg.						
13	Product R & D						
14	Sales Commission						
15	Sales Training						
16	Profit Sharing						
17	Total Adjustments						
18	Forecasted Demand						
19	Stockout Effect						
20	Forecasted Sales						

Sales Forecast Form

Market _____

(figures expressed in units)

		Year _____				Year ___	Year ___
		Qtr. 1	Qtr. 2	Qtr. 3	Qtr. 4	Total	Total
1	Previous Quarter Sales						
2	Previous Quarter Demand						
3	Customer Change						
4	Backorders						
5	Trend						
6	Seasonal						
7	Gross Domestic Prod.						
8	Pers. Consump. Exp.						
9	Household Forma.						
10	Price						
11	Advertising						
12	Sales Force Chg.						
13	Product R & D						
14	Sales Commission						
15	Sales Training						
16	Profit Sharing						
17	Total Adjustments						
18	Forecasted Demand						
19	Stockout Effect						
20	Forecasted Sales						

Production Plan Form
(Figures expressed in units)

			Year 2				Year 3	Year 4
			Qtr. 1	Qtr. 2	Qtr. 3	Qtr. 4		
1	Market 1	Sales Forecast						
2		Desired End Inventory						
3		Beginning Inventory						
4		Production Required						
5	Market 2	Sales Forecast						
6		Desired End Inventory						
7		Beginning Inventory						
8		Production Required						
9	Market 3	Sales Forecast						
10		Desired End Inventory						
11		Beginning Inventory						
12		Production Required						
13	**Total**	Production Required						
14		Productivity						
15		Hours Scheduled						
16		Prod. Force Required (number of persons)						
17		Prod. Force Change (number of persons)						
18	**Market 1 Allocation** (percentage)							
19	**Market 2 Allocation** (percentage)							
20	**Market 3 Allocation** (percentage)							

Production Plan Form

(Figures expressed in units)

			Year 2				Year 3	Year 4
			Qtr. 1	Qtr. 2	Qtr. 3	Qtr. 4		
1	Market 1	Sales Forecast						
2		Desired End Inventory						
3		Beginning Inventory						
4		Production Required						
5	Market 2	Sales Forecast						
6		Desired End Inventory						
7		Beginning Inventory						
8		Production Required						
9	Market 3	Sales Forecast						
10		Desired End Inventory						
11		Beginning Inventory						
12		Production Required						
13	**Total**	Production Required						
14		Productivity						
15		Hours Scheduled						
16		Prod. Force Required (number of persons)						
17		Prod. Force Change (number of persons)						
18	**Market 1 Allocation** (percentage)							
19	**Market 2 Allocation** (percentage)							
20	**Market 3 Allocation** (percentage)							

Raw Material Plan Form

		Year 2				Year 3	Year 4
		Qtr. 1	Qtr. 1	Qtr. 1	Qtr. 1		
1	Total Production Required (in units)						
2	Raw Material/unit (in lbs./unit)						
3	Raw Material Required (in millions of lbs.)						
4	Beginning Raw Material Inventory (millions)						
5	Raw Material Remaining After Production (millions)						
6	Raw Material Required Next Period (millions)						
7	Desired Ending Inventory Next Period (millions)						
8	Raw Material to Order This Period (millions)						
9	Process R. & D.						

Raw Material Plan Form

		Year 2				Year 3	Year 4
		Qtr. 1	Qtr. 1	Qtr. 1	Qtr. 1		
1	Total Production Required (in units)						
2	Raw Material/unit (in lbs./unit)						
3	Raw Material Required (in millions of lbs.)						
4	Beginning Raw Material Inventory (millions)						
5	Raw Material Remaining After Production (millions)						
6	Raw Material Required Next Period (millions)						
7	Desired Ending Inventory Next Period (millions)						
8	Raw Material to Order This Period (millions)						
9	Process R. & D.						

Human Resources Plan Form
(figures expressed in numbers of persons)

			Year 2				Year 3	Year 4
			Qtr 1	Qtr 2	Qtr 3	Qtr 4	Total	Total
1	**Market 1**	Sales Force						
2		Sales Trainees						
3		Proj. Termin.						
4		Adjusted Size						
5		Desired Size						
6		Req. Change						
7	**Market 2**	Sales Force						
8		Sales Trainees						
9		Proj. Termin.						
10		Adjusted Size						
11		Desired Size						
12	Change	Required						
13	**Market 3**	Sales Force						
14		Sales Trainees						
15		Proj. Termin.						
16		Adjusted Size						
17		Desired Size						
18		Req. Change						
19	**Production**	Prod. Force						
20		Proj. Termin.						
21		Adjusted Size						
22		Desired Size						
23		Req. Change						

Human Resources Plan Form

(figures expressed in numbers of persons)

			Year 2				Year 3	Year 4
			Qtr 1	Qtr 2	Qtr 3	Qtr 4	Total	Total
1	**Market 1**	Sales Force						
2		Sales Trainees						
3		Proj. Termin.						
4		Adjusted Size						
5		Desired Size						
6		Req. Change						
7	**Market 2**	Sales Force						
8		Sales Trainees						
9		Proj. Termin.						
10		Adjusted Size						
11		Desired Size						
12	Change	Required						
13	**Market 3**	Sales Force						
14		Sales Trainees						
15		Proj. Termin.						
16		Adjusted Size						
17		Desired Size						
18		Req. Change						
19	**Production**	Prod. Force						
20		Proj. Termin.						
21		Adjusted Size						
22		Desired Size						
23		Req. Change						

Wage and Salary Plan Form

		Year 2				Year 3	Year 4
		Qtr 1	Qtr 2	Qtr 3	Qtr 4	Total	Total
1	Sales Salary (In dollars/month)						
2	Sales Training (in thousands of dollars)						
3	Production Wage Rate (in dollars/hour)						
4	Production Training (in thousands of dollars)						
5	Profit Sharing (percentage)						

Wage and Salary Plan Form

		Year 2				Year 3	Year 4
		Qtr 1	Qtr 2	Qtr 3	Qtr 4	Total	Total
1	Sales Salary (In dollars/month)						
2	Sales Training (in thousands of dollars)						
3	Production Wage Rate (in dollars/hour)						
4	Production Training (in thousands of dollars)						
5	Profit Sharing (percentage)						

Cash Budget Form

			Year ___			Year ___	Year ___
		Qtr.1	Qtr.2	Qtr.3	Qtr.4	Total	Total
1	Accounts to be received						
2	Bank Loans						
3	Bond Sale Return						
4	Savings-- Interest and Withdrawal						
5	Plant and Equipment Sale						
6	Stock Sale Return						
7	Beginning Cash						
8	Total Sources						
9	Production Costs						
10	Marketing Costs						
11	Other Costs						
12	Dividends						
13	Loan Repayment						
14	Bonds Redeemed						
15	Income Taxes						
16	Profit sharing Cost						
17	Plant & Equipment Investment						
18	Savings Deposit						
19	Total Allocations						
20	Ending Cash Balance						

Cash Budget Form

		Qtr.1	Qtr.2	Qtr.3	Qtr.4	Year ___ ___ Total	Year ___ Total
1	Accounts to be received						
2	Bank Loans						
3	Bond Sale Return						
4	Savings-- Interest and Withdrawal						
5	Plant and Equipment Sale						
6	Stock Sale Return						
7	Beginning Cash						
8	Total Sources						
9	Production Costs						
10	Marketing Costs						
11	Other Costs						
12	Dividends						
13	Loan Repayment						
14	Bonds Redeemed						
15	Income Taxes						
16	Profit sharing Cost						
17	Plant & Equipment Investment						
18	Savings Deposit						
19	Total Allocations						
20	Ending Cash Balance						

Cost Estimates Form

		Year ___				Year ___	Year ___
		Qtr. 1	Qtr. 2	Qtr. 3	Qtr. 4	Total	Total
1	**Production**						
2	Labor						
3	Raw Material						
4	Maintenance						
5	Training						
6	Production Level Change.						
7	Equipment Replacement						
8	Total Production Cost						
9	**Marketing**						
10	Advertising						
11	Sales Salaries						
12	Sales Comm.						
13	Transportation						
14	Sales Training						
15	Sales Force Chgange						
16	Marketing Administration						
17	Total Marketing Cost						
18	**Other**						
19	Research & Development.						
20	Fin. Prod. Carrrying Cost						
21	Raw Mat Carrying Cost						
22	Bond Interest						
23	Bond Call Premium						
24	Loan Interest						
25	Other Administration						
26	Total Other Cost						

Cost Estimates Form

		Year ___				Year ___	Year ___
		Qtr. 1	Qtr. 2	Qtr. 3	Qtr. 4	Total	Total
1	**Production**						
2	Labor						
3	Raw Material						
4	Maintenance						
5	Training						
6	Production Level Change.						
7	Equipment Replacement						
8	Total Production Cost						
9	**Marketing**						
10	Advertising						
11	Sales Salaries						
12	Sales Comm.						
13	Transportation						
14	Sales Training						
15	Sales Force Chgange						
16	Marketing Administration						
17	Total Marketing Cost						
18	**Other**						
19	Research & Development.						
20	Fin. Prod. Carrrying Cost						
21	Raw Mat Carrying Cost						
22	Bond Interest						
23	Bond Call Premium						
24	Loan Interest						
25	Other Administration						
26	Total Other Cost						

Income Statement Form

		Year ___				Year ___	Year ___
		Qtr. 1	Qtr. 2	Qtr. 3	Qtr. 4	Total	Total
1	Gross Sales Revenue						
2	Beginning Inventory						
3	Total Production Cost						
4	Goods Available						
5	Ending Inventory						
6	Cost of Goods Sold						
7	Gross Profit						
8	Marketing Cost						
9	Profit on Sales						
10	Other Costs						
11	Other Income						
12	Net Profit Before Taxes						
13	Income Taxes						
14	Net Profit After Taxes						
15	Profit-Sharing Cost						
16	Net Income						
17	Dividends Paid						
18	Retained Earnings						

Income Statement Form

		Year ___				Year ___	Year ___
		Qtr. 1	Qtr. 2	Qtr. 3	Qtr. 4	Total	Total
1	Gross Sales Revenue						
2	Beginning Inventory						
3	Total Production Cost						
4	Goods Available						
5	Ending Inventory						
6	Cost of Goods Sold						
7	Gross Profit						
8	Marketing Cost						
9	Profit on Sales						
10	Other Costs						
11	Other Income						
12	Net Profit Before Taxes						
13	Income Taxes						
14	Net Profit After Taxes						
15	Profit-Sharing Cost						
16	Net Income						
17	Dividends Paid						
18	Retained Earnings						

Position Statement

		Year ___				Year ___	Year ___
		Qtr. 1	Qtr. 2	Qtr. 3	Qtr. 4	Total	Total
1	Cash Balance						
2	Accounts Receivable						
3	Finished Product Inventory						
4	Raw Material Inventory						
5	Savings Account Balance						
6	Total Current Assets						
7	Plant & Equipment Value						
8	Total Assets						
9	Bank Loan Balance						
10	Bonds Outstanding						
11	Capital Stock Value						
12	Accumulated Retained Earnings						
13	Total Stockholder's Equity						
14	Total Liabilities						

Position Statement

		Year ___				Year ___	Year ___
		Qtr. 1	Qtr. 2	Qtr. 3	Qtr. 4	Total	Total
1	Cash Balance						
2	Accounts Receivable						
3	Finished Product Inventory						
4	Raw Material Inventory						
5	Savings Account Balance						
6	Total Current Assets						
7	Plant & Equipment Value						
8	Total Assets						
9	Bank Loan Balance						
10	Bonds Outstanding						
11	Capital Stock Value						
12	Accumulated Retained Earnings						
13	Total Stockholder's Equity						
14	Total Liabilities						

Quarterly Decision Sheet

IDENTIFICATION

INDUSTRY	COMPANY	YEAR	QUARTER
_____	_____	_____	_____

MARKETING DECISIONS

PRODUCT PRICE (in dollars)

MARKET 1	MARKET 2	MARKET 3
_____.	_____.	_____.

ADVERTISING (thousands of $)

MARKET 1	MARKET 2	MARKET 3
_____.	_____.	_____.

SALES FORCE CHANGE (persons)

MARKET 1	MARKET 2	MARKET 3
_____	_____	_____

PRODUCT R&D (thousands $)   **SALES COMMISSION (percentage)**

PRODUCT R&D	SALES COMMISSION
_____.	_____._

PRODUCTION DECISIONS

PRODUCTION WORK WEEK (hrs./week)	LABOR FORCE CHANGE (persons)	ALLOCATION OF FINISHED PROD. (percentage to each market)			PROCESS R&D ($1000)	RAW MATERIAL ORDERED (millions lbs.)
		MARKET 1	MARKET 2	MARKET 3		
_____.	_____	_____.	_____.	_____.	_____.	_____.

HUMAN RESOURCE DECISIONS

SALES SALARY SHARING (dollars/mo.)	SALES TRAINING (thousands $)	PRODUCTION WAGE (dollars/hr.)	PROD. TRAINING (thousands $)	PROFIT (percentage)
_____.	_____.	_____.___	_____.	_____._

FINANCIAL DECISIONS

BONDS (thousands $)	BANK LOAN (thousands $)	DIVIDENDS PAID (thousands $)	STOCK ISSUED (1000s shares)	SAVINGS ACCOUNT (thousands $)
_____.	_____.	_____.	_____.	_____.

Quarterly Decision Sheet

IDENTIFICATION

INDUSTRY	COMPANY	YEAR	QUARTER
_____	_____	_____	_____

MARKETING DECISIONS

PRODUCT PRICE (in dollars)

MARKET 1	MARKET 2	MARKET 3
_____.	_____.	_____.

ADVERTISING (thousands of $)

MARKET 1	MARKET 2	MARKET 3
_____.	_____.	_____.

SALES FORCE CHANGE (persons)

MARKET 1	MARKET 2	MARKET 3
_____	_____	_____

PRODUCT R&D (thousands $)   **SALES COMMISSION (percentage)**

PRODUCT R&D (thousands $)	SALES COMMISSION (percentage)
_____.	_____._

PRODUCTION DECISIONS

PRODUCTION WORK WEEK (hrs./week)	LABOR FORCE CHANGE (persons)	ALLOCATION OF FINISHED PROD. (percentage to each market)			PROCESS R&D ($1000)	RAW MATERIAL ORDERED (millions lbs.)
		MARKET 1	MARKET 2	MARKET 3		
_____.	_____.	_____.	_____.	_____.	_____.	_____.

HUMAN RESOURCE DECISIONS

SALES SALARY SHARING (dollars/mo.)	SALES TRAINING (thousands $)	PRODUCTION WAGE (dollars/hr.)	PROD. TRAINING (thousands $)	PROFIT (percentage)
_____.	_____.	____.__	_____.	_____._

FINANCIAL DECISIONS

BONDS (thousands $)	BANK LOAN (thousands $)	DIVIDENDS PAID (thousands $)	STOCK ISSUED (1000s shares)	SAVINGS ACCOUNT (thousands $)
_____.	_____.	_____.	_____.	_____.

157

Quarterly Decision Sheet

IDENTIFICATION

INDUSTRY	COMPANY	YEAR	QUARTER
_____	_____	_____	_____

MARKETING DECISIONS

PRODUCT PRICE (in dollars)

MARKET 1	MARKET 2	MARKET 3
_____ .	_____ .	_____ .

ADVERTISING (thousands of $)

MARKET 1	MARKET 2	MARKET 3
_____ .	_____ .	_____ .

SALES FORCE CHANGE (persons)

MARKET 1	MARKET 2	MARKET 3
_____	_____	_____

PRODUCT R&D (thousands $)	SALES COMMISSION (percentage)
_____ .	_____ ._

PRODUCTION DECISIONS

PRODUCTION WORK WEEK (hrs./week)	LABOR FORCE CHANGE (persons)	ALLOCATION OF FINISHED PROD. (percentage to each market) MARKET 1	MARKET 2	MARKET 3	PROCESS R&D ($1000)	RAW MATERIAL ORDERED (millions lbs.)
_____ .	_____	_____ .	_____ .	_____ .	_____ .	_____ .

HUMAN RESOURCE DECISIONS

SALES SALARY SHARING (dollars/mo.)	SALES TRAINING (thousands $)	PRODUCTION WAGE (dollars/hr.)	PROD. TRAINING (thousands $)	PROFIT (percentage)
_____ .	_____ .	____ . __	_____ .	_____ ._

FINANCIAL DECISIONS

BONDS (thousands $)	BANK LOAN (thousands $)	DIVIDENDS PAID (thousands $)	STOCK ISSUED (1000s shares)	SAVINGS ACCOUNT (thousands $)
_____ .	_____ .	_____ .	_____ .	_____ .

Quarterly Decision Sheet

IDENTIFICATION

INDUSTRY	COMPANY	YEAR	QUARTER
_____	_____	_____	_____

MARKETING DECISIONS

PRODUCT PRICE (in dollars)

MARKET 1	MARKET 2	MARKET 3
_____.	_____.	_____.

ADVERTISING (thousands of $)

MARKET 1	MARKET 2	MARKET 3
_____.	_____.	_____.

SALES FORCE CHANGE (persons)

MARKET 1	MARKET 2	MARKET 3
_____	_____	_____

PRODUCT R&D (thousands $)   **SALES COMMISSION** (percentage)

PRODUCT R&D (thousands $)	SALES COMMISSION (percentage)
_____.	_____._

PRODUCTION DECISIONS

PRODUCTION WORK WEEK (hrs./week)	LABOR FORCE CHANGE (persons)	ALLOCATION OF FINISHED PROD. (percentage to each market) MARKET 1	MARKET 2	MARKET 3	PROCESS R&D ($1000)	RAW MATERIAL ORDERED (millions lbs.)
_____.	_____	_____.	_____.	_____.	_____.	_____.

HUMAN RESOURCE DECISIONS

SALES SALARY SHARING (dollars/mo.)	SALES TRAINING (thousands $)	PRODUCTION WAGE (dollars/hr.)	PROD. TRAINING (thousands $)	PROFIT (percentage)
_____.	_____.	_____.__	_____.	_____._

FINANCIAL DECISIONS

BONDS (thousands $)	BANK LOAN (thousands $)	DIVIDENDS PAID (thousands $)	STOCK ISSUED (1000s shares)	SAVINGS ACCOUNT (thousands $)
_____.	_____.	_____.	_____.	_____.